Where Are My Birth Parents?

Where Are My Birth Parents?

A Guide for Teenage Adoptees

Karen Gravelle
&
Susan Fischer

Walker and Company
New York

First published in the United States of America in 1993 by Walker Publishing Company, Inc.; first paperback edition published in 1995

Published simultaneously in Canada by Thomas Allen & Son Canada, Limited, Markham, Ontario

Library of Congress Cataloging-in-Publication Data
Gravelle, Karen.
Where are my birth parents? : a guide for teenage adoptees / Karen Gravelle and Susan Fischer.
p. cm.
Includes bibliographical references.
Summary: Discusses how and why adopted children may try to locate and get to know their birth parents and examines possible psychological benefits and problems associated with the process.
ISBN 0-8027-8257-4. — ISBN 0-8027-8258-2 (reinforced)
1. Birthparents—United States—Identification—Juvenile literature.   2. Adoptees—United States—Juvenile literature.   3. Children, Adopted—United States—Juvenile literature.   4. Adoption—United States—Psychological aspects—Juvenile literature.
[1. Birthparents.   2. Adoption.]   I. Fischer, Susan H.   II. Title.
HV875.55.G7   1993
362.7'34—dc20   92-34586
CIP
AC
ISBN 0-8027-7453-9 (paper)

Printed in the United States of America
Design by Ellen Levine

2   4   6   8   10   9   7   5   3   1

Contents

Acknowledgments

We would like to thank the many adoptees, birth parents, and adoptive parents who so openly shared their experiences with us. Many of the things they talked about were extremely painful to express, but they were willing to discuss these issues in order that adolescents who are adopted might benefit from what they have learned. Although we have changed their names to protect their privacy, their thoughts and feelings remain unaltered.

In addition we would like to express our appreciation to two professionals working in this field for their insights and assistance in writing this book. Many thanks to Mr. Joe Soll, C.S.W., director of Adoption Crossroads and director of CERA (Council for Equal Rights in Adoption) and Ms. Diane Mees of Adoption Crossroads, Westchester County, New York.

Introduction

ALTHOUGH many adoptees in the past have wanted to locate their birth parents, it is only recently that some adoptees have begun to feel comfortable acknowledging this desire. In ever-increasing numbers, they are coming to realize that the need to know their ethnic background and to connect with the mother and father who conceived them is normal, natural, and their right as human beings.

In spite of considerable media publicity surrounding adoptee-parent reunions, however, many adoptees either do not know that successful searching is possible or have no idea how to go about it.

As *Where Are My Birth Parents?* illustrates, teenagers can and do successfully search for their birth parents. Searching as an adolescent, however, is somewhat different from searching as an adult, partly because of legal restrictions and partly because teenagers are going through different life experiences.

Whereas adopted teenagers often think about their birth mothers, most don't actively begin searching until they are older. In addition to thinking that it is illegal for minors to search, many are too busy dealing with the issues of adolescence to take this on as well. Others simply don't feel the need to locate their birth parents.

Because so few teens have actually begun searching, many of the adoptees quoted in this book—Alicia, Maggie, Laura, Carol, Larry, Sharon, Robert, and Ed—are older. On the other hand, Chloe, Emily, and Selena, whose search experiences are presented in depth in chapter 7, were teenagers when they began to search for their birth mothers. Regardless of their age, however, all agreed that the issues surrounding adoption and search were similar.

Many adoptees are interested in finding their birth fathers as well as their birth mothers. For a number of reasons, however, a search usually focuses on the mother first. This is natural, since the major emotional connection of an infant and child is with its mother, not its father. Moreover, since she was the person who officially surrendered the child, she is the one most likely to be able to answer the adoptee's questions. Also, on a pragmatic level, the birth mother may be the only source of the father's name. Thus the mother often has to be found before a search for the father can begin.

Introduction

Finally, many adoptees assume their birth father was a creep. They conclude that if he hadn't abandoned their mother, they would not have had to be surrendered. Therefore, they may be reluctant to meet him.

By talking with their birth mother adoptees sometimes learn that their father didn't even know she was pregnant; perhaps he had been willing to marry her, but she declined. At this point, they often wish to search for him as well. In any event, most adoptees want to establish some relationship with their birth mother before trying to find their birth father.

For some of these same reasons, fewer birth fathers than birth mothers search for their children. Some birth fathers may not even know they have a child who was surrendered for adoption. Or, if they know, they are less likely than birth mothers to have necessary information such as the date and place of their child's birth. Finally, because they do not carry the child for nine months of their lives, it is easier for them to deny the painful feelings involved. However, many men are very distressed about having lost their children and search long and hard to find them.

Until recently, many more female than male adoptees have attempted to search for their birth mother. Often this desire intensifies when the adoptee becomes pregnant and begins to identify with how difficult it must have been for her mother to surrender her. Another reason may be that our society permits women to admit their emotional pain, including that surrounding their adoption.

Lately, however, many more boys and men have begun to search, although they tend to start at an older age than women. Larry is one of these men. When he was fourteen years old and only four feet six inches tall, he completely stopped growing. Alarmed, his adoptive parents took him to one of the best hospitals in the country to determine what was wrong.

"They said that I wasn't growing because I was chewing up all my energy worrying about something," Larry recalls. "I knew exactly what they were talking about! It was all this stuff about being adopted. But I couldn't tell my parents."

Fortunately, Larry started growing again. Other things changed as well. Now a psychotherapist who heads a search group in New York, Larry talks *a lot* about adoption. For him and many others, being able to express their feelings about being adopted has been a healthy and liberating experience.

If you are an adoptee, *Where Are My Birth Parents?* can help you understand similar emotions that you might have. For some, that may be as far as you wish to go right now. If you decide to search for your birth parents, however, this book will help you learn what to expect and guide you in beginning your search. Either way, the choice is up to you.

Chapter 1

Why Search?

I F you are an adoptee who wants to search for your birth parents, the question, "Why do you want to find your birth mother?" can seem a strange thing to be asked. It's not that you don't know how to respond. But the answer probably seems so obvious to you that you may wonder why anyone would bother to ask. "Because I want to know my mother, because I want to know where I came from, because I want to know who I am." If you are like most adoptees in search of your birth parents, that says it all.

But to many people who aren't adopted, this doesn't seem to answer their question. Obviously, you want to find your birth parents, but *why*? If you have adoptive parents who love you, why would you wish to find someone who gave you away? And how will meeting a stranger help you to know who you are—don't you know that already?

The difference in the way adoptees and nonadoptees look at this question is at the heart of why many adoptees wish to find their birth parents. To put it very simply, the life experience of most adoptees is profoundly different in many ways from the life experience of people who aren't adopted, although nonadoptees rarely recognize this difference.

Adoptees who wish to search for their birth parents are acutely aware of the difference, however. For them, something central in their lives is missing, something the rest of the world takes for granted. To find that missing piece, many are willing to engage in a long and frustrating search to locate their birth parents, and to risk being rejected by them again.

If you are an adoptee reading this book, you probably have a sense of what this missing piece is. If, on the other hand, you grew up with your biological parents, try to imagine what it would be like to go through your whole life never knowing anyone you were related to. Everyone else is connected by blood to someone. If you are not connected to anyone, where do you fit in the world?

Although many adoptees may not feel different from others when they are first told that they are adopted, they soon learn to feel this way. Ed, who is now a high school teacher in his early forties, still recalls the anger he felt when people asked him, "Is that your *real* mother? Who's your *real* mother?" "I always found that so offensive!" he says. Questions like these made it very clear that he was not like children who weren't adopted.

Other experiences also convey to adoptees that they are somehow outsiders. Very often, they don't look like other family members. They may notice on their own that other children resemble their parents while they do not, or playmates may ask them why they don't look like the rest of their family. When adoptees are of a different race from the people who adopted them, the difference is glaring and may invite comments to that effect from total strangers.

Maggie is also a high school teacher. Her adoptive parents, who thought they were infertile, had a biological child after they adopted her. "I really didn't feel that they loved my sister more, or that she was favored," Maggie says. But the fact that her sister resembled her parents, whereas she didn't, was painful. "There was always a pang of envy, when people would make conversation like, 'Bridget looks just like . . .' And I would feel left out. It wasn't something people did consciously to hurt me, but I was hurt by statements like that . . . statements in which I wasn't included, where I was left out somehow," she explains.

Like Maggie, Carol—now a lawyer in her late twenties—didn't look dramatically different from others in her family. But she had a similar longing to be told she resembled someone. "I wanted to look like someone very badly. I felt excluded from my family because I didn't," she remembers. "I used to stare at pictures from my mother's family and say, 'Oh, do you think I look like so-and-so?' That was always there very strongly for me."

If the adoptive family is closely connected to an ethnic culture that is very different from the adoptee's biological heritage, the sense of not really belonging in the family is accentuated. For example, Asian or Nordic children who are expected to identify with the Jewish culture, as Emily and Chloe were, are faced with an impossible task. Every time they entered a temple, heads turned and people asked who they were and why they were attending services.

Even when adoptees look like other family members, they are aware this is coincidental, not because of genetic similarities. Laura is a very attractive woman in her early thirties who looks as Italian as the rest of her family. In fact, Laura resembles her adoptive parents more than their biological daughter does. However, both she and her mother feel awkward when strangers comment on this similarity. They know these statements are based on the assumption that Laura inherited her appearance from her mother—something both of them know isn't true. Thus, adoptees who resemble others in their families may feel almost like frauds.

4

Why Search?

Unlike Emily and Chloe, Maggie identified strongly with her adoptive family's Irish-American culture. But even though she loved the music, the Irish brogue of her mother, and Saint Patrick's Day, she felt she didn't have the right to claim the culture as her own. Clearly, if her own background turned out to be something very different, she could hardly call herself Irish, no matter how much she valued the culture.

For some adoptees, the differences they experience can go even deeper than a feeling of not really belonging in the family or the problem of trying to identify with an ethnic background that may not be theirs. If you are like these adoptees, you may even have wondered at times if you really exist. Crazy as this may seem, the feeling is normal for someone who has been adopted. People who are not adopted know they were born because others in their family witnessed the event. They grow up hearing stories about their birth. Adoptees never have this experience. They don't know anyone who was present when they were born. Since no one can actually confirm the fact that they were born, how do they know it is so? Of course, intellectually adoptees realize they must have been born, since this is the only way they could have come to be. But on an emotional level, it sometimes feels as if they dropped down to Earth from another planet. If they aren't connected biologically to anyone else, if no one witnessed their birth, do they really exist?

Where Are My Birth Parents?

When adoptees try to discuss their feelings of being different from others in the family, their parents frequently respond by saying, "We love you as if you were our own child," or, if the parents also have biological children, "There is no difference between you and your brothers and sisters—we love you all the same."

What these parents don't understand is that their adopted children are not talking about love, they are talking about difference. Obviously, for adopted children who feel less loved *because* they are adopted, love and difference are intertwined. But even adopted children who feel *more* loved than their parents' biological children can still feel different. They feel different because, in a fundamental sense, they are. This is not the same as feeling unloved.

There are certainly adoptees who may not relate to the experiences described so far. Being adopted may not have caused them to feel that something is missing, that they are different from other people, or that they have an emotional need to locate their birth parents.

But if you are an adoptee who has picked this book to read, there is a reason you've made that choice. Chances are, some of the feelings expressed above sound familiar to you. Like others, you may feel that something about your sense of yourself is missing; that connecting with your birth mother or birth parents will help you feel the same continuity with your ancestors, with your beginnings, and with your ethnic culture that nonadoptees feel; that by knowing where you came from and what your biological heritage is, you will know where you fit in the world; and that, by meeting your birth mother, the person who witnessed your birth, you will finally have proof that you exist. These are all good reasons for wanting to find your birth parents.

So, of course, is wanting your medical history. Though most adoptees would probably like to know this information, it is rarely a primary reason for wanting to find one's birth parents. It is, however, a very safe thing to say and something that makes sense to nonadoptees.

As Carol explains, "It can be the first layer of reasons to get into [searching] but there really is a lot of other stuff going on. The medical aspect is the easiest to acknowledge. Everyone sympathizes with it, especially as more and more information is out in the press about how important family history is. It's not disloyal to your adoptive parents, and it's not intruding on birth mothers."

Part of the "other stuff" that Carol refers to is the hope that finding one's birth mother will help to heal old emotional wounds. Upon the advice of adoption agencies, most adoptive parents in this country tell their children about the adoption when the youngsters are two to four years old. Usually, adoptees are also told that they were "chosen" and are therefore "special."

While this information might not make much of a conscious impact upon such young children, when they reach six or seven adoptees begin to realize that they had to have been abandoned first before they could be chosen. With the understanding that their adoptive parents are not their biological parents, they may also feel that they have lost this set of "real" parents as well.

As they learn more about adoption in general and their parents' reasons for adopting in particular, adoptees may come to feel that being "chosen" is not all it's cracked up to be. First, in most instances, it's not true. With the exception of couples who already have biological children and decide to adopt a child who needs a home, most parents do not really choose to adopt. In the vast majority of cases they are told they are unable to have children of their own, and they decide to adopt because it's the only way they will be able to raise a child.

Not only do most adoptive parents not really choose to adopt, usually they do not even choose which individual child they will adopt. Especially if they want a healthy white infant, they consider themselves lucky to get any child that's available—hardly much of a reason for the adoptee to feel "special."

For many adoptees, believing that they have been abandoned by their original parents, that someone made a conscious choice not to keep them, creates a deep wound that can result in low self-esteem, insecurity about their place in their adoptive families, and difficulty in forming close relationships. Often they be-

8

lieve something must be wrong with them or that they are somehow unlovable. Otherwise, their birth mother would not have given them away.

As Alicia expresses it, "One of the problems about being adopted is that you're illegitimate. You were given away, so why is anybody going to want you? It's a secret almost that you're supposed to keep."

Since they don't understand why they were relinquished in the first place, they may fear that it could always happen again. As a result, many adoptees either believe that they have to be especially good to ensure they won't be surrendered again, or they become rebellious, continually testing their adoptive parents to see if they will be rejected.

Alicia was one of the good children. "I wanted to make sure that everything was fine and that we were a happy family," she says, "because it felt like I had something at stake, like I could lose them. I think there's always a subconscious feeling that it could happen. I didn't do anything when I was born, but something had to have been wrong with me for someone to give me away."

Although others may not be able to tell from your behavior that you have these feelings, chances are that, if you're adopted, it hurts to know that your biological parents didn't keep you. Even if you feel very secure in your adoptive parents' love and know they won't abandon you, you probably still wonder why your birth mother didn't seem to want you.

For Maggie, this issue is very painful. *"Why?"* she asks. "That's the big question. Why? Why was I rejected? It's very hard for most people to conceive of a person surrendering this adorable little infant, this real helpless little infant."

Robert was adopted over forty years ago but, like many other adoptees, he still suffers the effects of having been surrendered. It angers him that nonadoptees don't realize how damaging this event can be. "Adoption is a tragedy," he says.

It's not that he thinks children shouldn't be adopted, but he objects to the way the process is handled. "I think the biggest problem is how we deal with adoption in this country," he adds. "People aren't willing to admit that a significant loss has occurred. I don't believe anyone can lose their mother and father and not have some negative effects. There is a sense of loss, there's a grieving that needs to occur.

"You know," he continues, "if a child's parents are killed when he is two days old, everyone sees that as a tragedy. But if the child is surrendered, no one sees that as a tragedy. I wish the parents that do adopt could somehow try to acknowledge that this is a bad thing that happened."

Your adoptive parents can help you with many things, but if you need to know why your birth mother surrendered you, being able to ask her directly may be the only way you can understand what happened.

Searching for your birth parents can also help you gain a sense of control over your life. If you are adopted, all of the decisions around your adoption—probably the most important event in your life—have been made and continue to be made by other people. Your birth mother decided to surrender you, your adoptive parents decided to adopt you, the adoption agency decided which family you would go to, and the courts have decided whether or not you can have vital information about yourself. The only one who never got and still doesn't get to make a decision about your adoption is you.

It can feel very strange to know that the whole course of your life could have been different if you had been adopted by someone else. Sharon is now a single mother in her twenties. The way she describes it, "My father told me, 'We picked you out of a group of kids.' I felt like it was an auction. If they didn't come around someone else would have, and I would've had a different life. Whoever came, came."

Knowing that the most basic facts of their lives have been determined by the whims of others, some adoptees become very passive about things over which they actually do have control. Because they had no part in the most important decision in their lives, some find themselves either reluctant or lacking in the confidence

11

to make other decisions. By searching for their birth parents, they have the chance to actively take control over the facts of their adoption and to feel that their lives are in their own hands, not someone else's.

Although younger children often fantasize about their original parents, most adoptees do not begin to consider actually searching for their birth parents until they are teenagers or adults. There are many reasons why this issue becomes important for adolescent adoptees, even if they don't actively start searching until later in life.

Defining who you are as an individual is a major part of being an adolescent. Like everyone else, adoptees need to know where they came from in order to begin to develop a sense of who they are. Because they lack the basic knowledge of their biological roots, teenage adoptees have a harder time trying to form their own sense of identity.

Separating from their parents also can be more difficult for adolescents who are adopted. While other teenagers struggle to establish space between themselves and their parents, many adoptees feel a little too separate to begin with, and it is hard to separate if you aren't solidly connected first. Moreover, even if they successfully separate from their adoptive parents, adoptees have a set of phantom parents—their birth parents—whom they haven't even met yet, much less connected with.

Finally, adolescents are now entering into sexual and romantic relationships themselves, and this often stirs up questions about their own conception. Many adoptees had, or believe they had, birth mothers who were quite young. As they approach the age that their mother was when they were surrendered, girls who have been adopted begin to identify, or try to identify, with her experience.

Besides the many good reasons to search for your birth parents, there are other reasons that are not so helpful. Adolescence can be a rough time for the relationship between you and your parents, regardless of whether you are adopted or not. If you are adopted, however, you may fantasize that life with your "real" parents could never be as bad as life with the parents you "got stuck with." Searching for your birth parents because you are angry at your adoptive parents or because you think finding your birth parents will solve all your problems is a bad idea indeed. Finding your birth parents won't solve the difficulties you face, and you are very likely to end up disappointed and hurt.

Deciding to search is serious business and your decision should be based on healthy reasons, not on anger or a desire to escape. Not only is searching a long and difficult process, but it will stir up a lot of powerful—

and sometimes painful—emotions. The fact that you are an adolescent doesn't mean you can't handle these feelings. But, like the adult adoptees who search, you will need a lot of emotional support as you look for, and hopefully find, your birth parents.

Chapter 2

Telling Your Parents

DECIDING to search for your birth parents is a big and often frightening step. If you are like many adoptees, the next step—telling your adoptive parents about the decision—may be equally scary.

Will my parents be hurt by my desire to find my birth mother? Will they think I'm abandoning them? Will they think I'm ungrateful? Will they still love me? How can I make them understand how important this is to me? What do I do if they don't want me to search? If you are considering searching for your birth mother, you are probably struggling with at least one of these issues.

Not only are most adoptees reluctant to upset their parents but many are afraid that their decision to search may completely destroy the relationships they have with their families. Adoptees often fear that they may inadvertently do something that results in their being "given up" again. If you sometimes feel this way, telling your parents that you wish to find your birth mother may seem very risky.

Helping your parents understand why you wish to search can be even more complicated if you are an adolescent. Like adolescents who aren't adopted, you may find that your relationship with your parents has become more difficult than it used to be. It's important to recognize that you and your parents will probably be coming from very different positions regarding your desire to search. Understanding what both of you may be experiencing will give you a better chance of getting through to them.

Although they may not show it, your parents, like the parents of adolescents who aren't adopted, often suffer a sense of loss and insecurity during your teenage years. While they know that you need to break away from them in order to become independent, this does not change the fact that they are losing you—not as a person but as a child—to adulthood. If they have done their job well, they will always have your love and respect. But, *especially* if they have done their job well, their role in your life as guiding and protective adults will soon be over.

Unfortunately, your parents must deal with the loss of a major role in their own lives at the same time that their sense of self-worth is taking a significant beating. In an effort to define their own values, adolescents can be extremely critical of the values their parents have tried to instill. Again, while most parents understand intellectually that you must challenge their ideas if you are going to figure out what it is you truly believe, they often can't help feeling that they and everything they stand for are being rejected.

Few adoptive parents—whatever their child's age—are thrilled by the idea of adoptees wishing to search for their birth mothers. Even when they have good, close relationships with their children, adoptive parents usually feel at least somewhat threatened by their child's intense desire to meet his or her birth mother. While the burning question for the adoptee is, "Did she [my birth mother] love me?" the question that haunts adoptive parents is, "Will our child love her more than us?"

When an adoptee's desire to search surfaces during adolescence, it frequently coincides with parents' feelings that they are already being rejected by their child. Now, in addition to the normal loss of their adolescent to adulthood, they face the prospect of losing him or her to *another parent*. Far from being part of a natural process, this loss may seem both very unfair and unnatural.

Since few adoptive parents are themselves adoptees, they usually have little understanding of the degree to which being adopted can affect a person's entire

17

life. From their perspective, they have done their best to provide you with a stable and loving family. Your wish to know your birth mother may sometimes be interpreted as a statement that the love and care that they have provided have been completely inadequate and that only your birth mother can give you what you really need.

In terms of the sense of groundedness that most adoptees are seeking, this is true—only a connection with your birth mother can provide that particular need. However, this is *not* the same as saying that you have any intention of "trading in" your parents for a birth mother—something they may need help in understanding.

Making things even more difficult for parents is the fact that their child's announcement that he or she wishes to search often comes as a bolt out of the blue. Since many adoptees seem comfortable acknowledging to others that they are adopted, parents generally assume that this means they have accepted the fact and have no problems around the issue.

To discover that this is not the case—that you may be experiencing a sense of pain and incompleteness from not knowing your birth mother—can be a real shock. Parents of a teenager, regardless of whether their child was adopted or not, typically struggle with the fear that they are losing touch with their child. The revelation that you may have very different feelings about being adopted than they ever imagined tends to make that concern worse.

In addition to the fear that they may be replaced in your heart by another, more primary, parent, your desire to connect with your birth mother may stir up other painful feelings for your parents as well. Although there are many exceptions, most parents adopt because they are unable to have children. In our society as well as most others, infertility is a deeply stigmatizing condition, attacking a person's most basic sense of worth as a male or female.

If your parents were unable to have children, they may have experienced a series of extremely distressing failures to conceive and/or several emotionally wrenching miscarriages before deciding to adopt. If so, that probably was a time in their lives they wish to forget. Unfortunately, your search for your birth mother can't help but remind them of this painful period. Some parents have a hard time handling these upsetting memories even when their adopted children are adults and the events that caused so much unhappiness occurred decades ago.

Finally, like adoptees and birth mothers, adoptive parents are handicapped in responding to their child's wish to search by the fact that they have no guidelines as to how to handle either their own or your feelings. On the contrary, most adoptive parents were led to believe it would be impossible for adoptees or birth parents to search and, thus, are completely unprepared to deal with your desire to find your birth mother.

Meanwhile, as a teenager, you are probably busy dealing with issues of your own. Two of the primary concerns of adolescents are separating from their parents and establishing their own independent identity. Separating from parents is never easy, but it can be even harder for teenagers who are adopted. Unlike adolescents who are not adopted, many adoptees feel uncomfortably different from, rather than too closely connected with, others in their family.

Thus, for teenage adoptees, the sense of having a solid family base that is unconditionally there for you may not be as strong as that experienced by nonadoptees. As a result, the normal adolescent actions of challenging your parents or taking positions that might displease them can be more difficult for you than for other teenagers.

Most teenage adoptees are well aware that their desire to search for their birth parents may be interpreted by their adoptive parents as a kind of rejection. Since they are acutely aware of how painful rejection can be, adoptees are often reluctant to inflict that pain on someone else, particularly a parent whom they love. In addition, adoptees sometimes secretly fear that their parents will respond to feeling rejected by rejecting them in return. If this sounds like something you've

worried about, approaching your parents about your
wish to search can be very frightening.

Because of these concerns, many adolescent adoptees are afraid to rock the boat further by announcing
that they wish to search for their birth mothers. If you
are a teenager who wants to find your birth parents, is
it better not to mention this to your adoptive parents
and just search on your own? Or perhaps to wait until
you are legally an adult?

Absolutely not! If it is important for you to search,
or if you are even thinking about doing so, there are
many good reasons for telling your parents, in spite of
the anxiety this may cause you both. First, on a practical level, few search groups or registry services allow
adolescents to participate without their parents' consent, and attempting to search on your own is very
difficult.

But this is probably the least significant reason for
sharing your feelings with your parents. More important, as your parents, they love you and can be a big
source of emotional support during the many ups and
downs you will experience as you go through the search
process. For example, just knowing they are there for
you can make it easier for you to handle the fear that
your birth mother may reject you.

Second, most adolescents want very much to be
recognized as individuals in their own right. If you feel
a need to connect with your birth mother, this is a very

important part of who you are as a person. Unless one or both of your parents are adopted themselves, they probably don't have a clue about this aspect of you. Thus they don't really know who you are—and they won't unless you tell them. If you hold back this information, you are robbing yourself of a chance to be understood and your parents of the opportunity to really know you.

However, don't expect your parents' feelings of being threatened to vanish simply because you reassure them of your love. Although they will certainly need this reassurance, and it will help, feelings don't just disappear because we want them to. As you know from your own experience, fears can't be wished away; they can only be acknowledged and dealt with.

For everyone—adoptees, birth mothers, and adoptive parents—fear is a big part of the search process. This is only natural, since everyone involved has so much at stake. It is generally helpful to your parents if they can talk to you about their fears. This does *not* mean, however, that you are responsible for helping your parents deal with their feelings or for making them feel better. That is their job. All you can do is to let them know you understand what they may be going through and that you care about their concerns.

Many adoptees feel that they need to be especially "good" and avoid causing problems for others, particularly their families. If this describes you, it may be hard

Telling Your Parents

to believe that it is not up to you to make your parents comfortable with your desire to search. Not only isn't this your responsibility, but you probably can't alleviate all of your parents' anxieties about your search no matter what you do. Even parents who understand why their child needs to connect with his or her birth mother and are genuinely supportive of the search are likely to feel threatened at times. Just as you may have conflicting emotions about searching for your birth parents, your adoptive parents will have ambivalent feelings about the experience too. This is to be expected, and it's all right.

Most search support groups welcome adoptive parents as well as adoptees and birth parents. Being part of a group can help your parents gain a better understanding of adoptees' and birth parents' need to search. At the same time, they have the chance to get support and help in handling their own feelings.

All this may sound fine for adoptees who have close relationships with their parents, but what if your relationship with one or both of your parents isn't that great? It may be hard for you to imagine them being supportive of you, much less being willing to accept support from you.

Unfortunately, while many parents are supportive of their child's search for his or her birth mother, some are not. When the adoptee is a teenager, this reluctance may arise in part from a concern that you are too young to handle the emotional pitfalls involved. In this case, your parents may become more comfortable with the idea when you are a few years older. In extreme cases, however, the relationship between an adoptee and his or her parents can become severely strained by the adoptee's desire to search. But it's important to keep in mind that this is rare.

Even if your relationship with your parents is rocky at best, this does not necessarily mean that they won't support you in your search. Sometimes, parents can surprise you.

Laura had every reason to believe that her adoptive mother would be angered by her desire to search. Although she had a good relationship with her father, Laura and her mother had never gotten along—in fact, she couldn't remember her mother ever telling her that she loved her. Because Laura was over twenty-one and did not need her parents' permission to search, she didn't let them know what she was doing until after she had located her birth parents. When she finally got up the courage to speak to her adoptive mother, it was with the fear that what she had to say might sever their relationship completely.

"I was *so terrified* to tell them! It was twice as bad as picking up the telephone to call [my birth mother]," she recalls. But, amazingly, both her father *and her mother* were supportive of what she had done.

"My mother . . . it was as if she knew before I even

got the words out. I think as a mother and as a woman who's both had a child and adopted a child, I think she really understood the need to do this and was almost waiting for me to say I was going to do it," Laura remembers. "She said she was *happy* for me. She said she felt that roots are important and that I had the *right* to know these things. And that it was *normal* to want to know these things. I was stunned! Really, really stunned," she adds. "I was just taken aback."

Not only was Laura relieved and elated, but her mother's response gave her a new perspective on their relationship. "When she reacted that way, I was *so happy*! I really felt like, 'Oh, my God! She understands me and cares about me more than I ever realized!' " Since then, her mother has showed signs of being a little threatened by Laura's newfound relationship with her birth mother, but Laura sees that as an indication that at least she's important enough to her mother that her mother doesn't want to lose her.

Surprisingly, although both adoptees and adoptive parents worry that the search will somehow damage their relationship with each other, the opposite is more likely to be true. Adoptees and their adoptive parents who struggle through the search process together usually find their relationship is greatly strengthened— even when it wasn't that good to start out with.

Emily, Chloe, and Selena, whose search experiences are presented in chapter 7, had difficult relationships with their adoptive mothers. In all three cases, however, their mothers really came through for them in supporting their search. Although Selena found her birth mother, while Emily and Chloe have not yet been successful, all three now have close relationships with their adoptive mothers—relationships that grew directly out of the search process.

There are several reasons why searching generally enhances the relationship between adoptees and their parents. First, finding out who they are and where they fit in the world increases the self-confidence and self-esteem of adoptees. And confident people, secure in who they are, usually find it easier to relate to others, including their parents.

Second, as a result of the search process, the adoption itself ceases to be a taboo subject within the family. Although the fact of the adoption is acknowledged in most adoptive families, any discussion of the feelings or circumstances surrounding it tends to be off-limits. The inability to talk about these things keeps family members apart. When barriers to sharing their feelings about adoption disappear, adoptees and their parents often find themselves drawing closer emotionally.

Finally, adoptive parents who help their child search are clearly doing so out of concern for their child's best interests. Adoptees are usually well aware that their parents make this effort in spite of considerable pain and anxiety and recognize it for what it is—a gift of love.

As Alicia says, "My mother helped me. She loved me enough that instead of saying no and being too scared, she said, 'Yeah, I'm going to help you if that's what you want to do.' My mom and dad helped me because they loved me and because it was something I needed. That's what it's all about!"

Chapter 3

Searching

THE major obstacle you will face in searching for your birth parents is the fact that in all states except Alaska, Kansas, and Hawaii, your birth and adoption records are legally sealed. Fortunately, however, there are many other sources that can give you information about your origins.

Surprisingly, one of these sources may be your adoptive parents. In addition to the reasons discussed in chapter 2, there are many practical reasons for telling them that you want to search. First, your parents may have more information regarding your adoption and your birth mother than you are aware of.

Some adoptive parents are reluctant to approach their children with what they know for fear that this will be upsetting and stir up difficult feelings for everyone. If your parents feel this way, they may be waiting for you to take the initiative, assuming that you will ask for the information when you are emotionally ready for it. Thus, if you avoid talking with them about your wish to search because you are worried about how they will react, you may miss some crucial information that could make your search a lot easier.

When Laura finally found out that she was of Irish and Jewish descent, she shared this information with her adoptive parents. To her shock, they already knew. "I asked why, in all those years, they never said anything," Laura recalls. "And their response was, 'You never asked.'"

Although Laura's parents rarely volunteered information about her adoption, they had always answered the few questions she asked. But because it hadn't occurred to her that they might have this kind of information, she never brought the topic up.

In most cases, your parents will have a limited amount of information they can give you because they were told very little about your birth mother and her circumstances when they adopted you. Although this is frustrating, the fact that they can't tell you much isn't all bad. You can use the extra time to begin to prepare emotionally for searching and for eventually meeting your birth mother.

On the other hand, in some cases, your parents may actually have all the facts you need to find your birth mother, particularly if your adoption was handled privately. If they are willing to give you this information, your response may be to try to make contact with her immediately. After all, that's why you started searching in the first place, right?

Tempting as it may be, however, you should *not* race right out to call your birth mother. You need to slow down and give yourself time to prepare emotionally to meet her. This includes exploring your expectations, thinking about the possible results of the phone call for both you and your birth mother, and just considering what it means to you that you finally have her name. Adoptees who have found their birth parents agree that the success of their reunions depended on how ready they were to handle their feelings, and that getting ready required a lot of time and work.

One of the best ways to prepare is to join a search group. Located in many cities throughout the country, these groups are led by individuals with extensive experience in searching. Adoptees searching for their birth parents, birth mothers searching for children they surrendered, and adoptive parents whose children are searching are all welcome to attend. As a teenager, however, you will have to have your adoptive parents' permission to join.

Although the schedule and format may vary, most groups meet once a week. Meetings generally begin with an open rap session, where adoptees and birth parents discuss their feelings about being adopted or surrendering their child, their fears about searching, the difficulties they are encountering in their searches, fantasies and expectations they have about reunion, and the process of reestablishing a relationship with their birth parent or child after many years of separation. Adoptive parents, on the other hand, may talk about their fears of losing their children to a birth parent or about their frustration in not being able to provide them with important information about their origins.

While the rap session is usually open to individuals who are not yet group members but are testing the waters to see if the group is something they might wish to become involved in, the part of the group devoted to search techniques and search help is restricted to official group members.

Depending on the particular group, some meetings may be actual psychotherapy sessions in which members work more deeply on the problems adoption has caused in their relationships with others, their self-image, and other important issues. In addition, some groups also sponsor weekend retreats to delve further into these areas.

If you feel confused about being adopted or about your desire to search, this is a good reason for attending such a group. Are you hoping to find a new family because you and your adoptive parents are arguing a lot? Are you angry at your birth mother and want to let her know this? It is important that you take a close look at your motivation for searching and what you hope the outcome will be. Discussing your fantasies is an important step in this process, whether you are looking for factual information or for an actual reunion. Talking with others who are struggling with some of the same questions and feelings that you may be experiencing can help you sort these things out.

Although adoptees enter the search process to learn who they are, they often don't realize that finding their birth parents may mean giving up a part of their self-image. Ed has always pictured himself as an orphan, as someone alone in the world. While this image saddens him, it's central to his view of himself and something that he is very used to. When Ed started to search, he realized that his self-image would have to change if he found his birth parents, for he would no longer be an orphan. "What would I do in that case?" he asks. "How would I adjust to a new image? It's real hard for me."

Searching is often a long and frustrating process, and one that invariably stirs up many upsetting feelings. Ed decided to search after he met someone who had successfully located a sister who had been adopted. "I was all set to do it," he says, "and a couple of days later, I was teaching a class when I began to have chest pains, heart palpitations, and sweating. I thought I was having a heart attack!"

The school raced him to the doctor. As it turned

out, Ed's symptoms were the result of a panic attack brought on by emotions that surfaced when he finally decided to search. Although most people do not have reactions as extreme as Ed's, many experience significant anxiety about delving into their past and about facing the possibility of being rejected by their birth mother a second time. These fears are to be expected, and helping adoptees to deal with these feelings is part of what a search group is for.

While your parents and friends can be an important source of support because they know you and care about you, they probably don't know what it feels like to be in your shoes. Getting emotional support from other adoptees who are going through what you are makes search groups especially valuable. As Ed explains, "In the group, we all have the experience of being adopted, so there's this bond. We've always felt so different from other people, we've been so good and pretended we were really someone else, that it didn't bother us, that we were really grateful, the whole thing. To be with other people who know just what it's like is tremendously freeing."

Another important reason for attending a group is that it offers you the opportunity to meet birth mothers. Most adoptees have preconceived notions about what birth mothers are like. Some of these images can be very negative—druggie, whore, low-life—reflecting both the stigma attached to having a child out of wedlock and the anger adoptees may feel toward their own birth mothers.

When Alicia heard that the search group she was planning to join admitted birth mothers, she was taken aback. "I thought, 'Oh, my God! What's a birth mother going to be like?' But then I met Gloria and she was sweet and wonderful and sincere. And I was dumbfounded! It was like 'Oh, my gosh! They're just like we are!' Except the other end, you know. And I think that really, really helped a lot."

A chance encounter with a birth mother changed Carol's perception of what her own mother might be like. "What made me decide to search was my first contact with a birth mother," she says. "She told me about finding her son and what that had meant to her. That was the first time that it hit me that there could be someone out there who wanted to know how I was, who might want to meet me, instead of just trying to forget me."

Later, birth mothers in her support group helped to pull Carol through the agonizing time after her own birth mother hung up when Carol first called her. "When that happened, I was able to get on the phone and call a couple of birth mothers I knew," she recalls. "And they could say, 'Relax! This is probably what she's going through, and her reaction is natural.' " With help in understanding that her birth mother's response was not necessarily the rejection she thought it was, Carol was able to try again—this time with success.

Group members can also help you anticipate various scenarios and offer suggestions as to how to handle them. You can practice your initial telephone call to your birth mother with someone in the group, thinking of all the possible responses your mother may make and deciding what to do in each case.

At various points in their search, most adoptees feel overwhelmed by the adoption system and the many concrete difficulties that they come up against. Another major reason for joining a search group is to gain access to search techniques and strategies that will help you work your way through these obstacles. Because adoption laws vary greatly from state to state, you will need the help of people who understand the situation where you live. Group leaders know the ins and outs of negotiating with institutions in your area and may have established relationships with agency employees who will be more responsive to your requests for information.

Should you go to the meetings alone? Attending a search group can stir up powerful feelings about being adopted that you may not have been aware you had, and the anger and sadness that can surface sometimes seem limitless and overwhelming. Depending on your relationship with your family, you may have had more or less help in understanding these painful and confusing emotions. But, in any event, hearing a group of people

openly discuss their feelings about being adopted—
probably for the first time in your life—is likely to be
both exciting and frightening. For this reason, it is recommended that you attend your first meeting with
someone you trust. After that, you can decide whether
you wish to continue to go with someone or attend by
yourself.

To locate a search group near you, contact the
Council for Equal Rights in Adoption (their address is
provided in "For More Information" at the back of the
book), or consult some of the books suggested under
"For Further Reading."

If there is no search group in your area, or if your
parents are unwilling to let you join one, you can still
begin to prepare emotionally for searching. Even if your
parents aren't comfortable with the idea of a search
group, they may be willing to let you go into therapy
with a psychotherapist or counselor who is particularly
sensitive to the issues of adoption.

You can also start reading. Listed in the back of
this book are books that can be helpful to you as you
explore your reasons for wanting to search and your
feelings about being adopted. *Remember, the physical
search, as tough as it can be, is actually the easy part.
The emotional part is much more difficult.* Thus, the
sooner you start dealing with these issues, the better.

Whether you are working on your own or through
a group, the next step is to contact the agency that han-

dled your adoption and request your nonidentifying information. Again, as an adolescent, you will need your parents' permission to obtain this material.

Your nonidentifying information may include facts about your birth mother's health history, physical description, religion, educational background, occupation, interests, talents, existence of extended family, the circumstances surrounding the adoption, and why she had to surrender you. Some information about your birth father may also be included. What is *not* a part of your nonidentifying information is your birth mother's (or father's) name and address.

Nonidentifying information is valuable in two ways. First, it helps to give you a better understanding about your background. Second, it provides you with beginning clues to use in locating your birth mother.

Getting her nonidentifying information allowed Maggie to feel that she truly belonged to the culture she loved. Having grown up in an Irish-American household she, like the rest of her adoptive family, had very strong ties to the Irish culture. Thus, learning that her birth mother was born in Ireland was the best news she could have received.

"I was really thrilled when I saw that!" she says. "It made me feel great, because I always *wanted* to be Irish! I like the fact that there was a very strong ethnic piece to my growing up, so I was really glad. It was like, 'Oh, all along I had a *right* to celebrate Saint Patrick's Day!'

"I was very anxious to share this with people that I loved. It was very important. I remember getting the letter and reading it and rereading it . . . just feeling very happy, like I had won the lottery. I got on the phone and started telling everyone, 'I found out about my birth mother and I look like her and she was Irish!'

"The word is *liberating*! That's the way I felt. I felt very empowered with this knowledge!"

Most adoptees are thrilled to learn something factual about their birth mother. As Carol says, "When you've had nineteen years of virtually no information, and then you get two and a half pages, it's such an increase that it seems like a lot. So, for a while, I was satisfied with it."

After knowing little or nothing at all about your birth mother for most of your life, suddenly learning something *real* can have a dramatic impact. You'll probably need time to integrate this information into your previous ideas about her and your fantasies of where you came from.

With your parents' consent, you can also place your name in a reunion registry. Most registries are private, but a few states have established their own. A registry is a computerized cross-indexing system containing vi-

Searching

tal statistics of adoptees and birth parents for possible matching. In most cases adoptees do not know their original names, and birth parents do not know the adotive names of the children they surrendered for adoption. They do know the sex of the child, the date of birth, and the place of birth, however.

If a mother who gave up a child and an adoptee with matching information have both registered, the registry will put them in contact with each other. Adoptees over eighteen years of age and birth parents who have surrendered children that are now eighteen years or older can register. There is usually a small fee, or the registration may be included in the support group's membership fee.

Your nonidentifying information and the facts provided by your parents give you a place to start your search. Adoptees determined to find their birth parents can often make Sherlock Holmes look like an amateur. Using her nonidentifying information, Carol created a profile of her birth mother. Since her mother had been referred to the adoption agency by a nearby youth program, Carol guessed that she must have lived in the surrounding area. She also knew her birth mother's father was a contractor and that her mother was the youngest of a very large family. With that information, Carol was able to rule out some of the more expensive neighborhoods in the vicinity, figuring that the family was unlikely to be well-to-do.

She also knew her mother's age when she gave birth to Carol, so she was able to determine when her mother had graduated from high school. Her next step was to go through yearbooks for that year from high schools in the neighborhoods she thought her mother might have lived in. Combining this with her nonidentifying information, Carol then made a list of possibilities. The last, and hardest step, was finding out what her own original name had been. Once she had that information, it was easy to match her original last name with one on her list.

Carol was lucky in a few respects. First, her mother was from the same area where the adoption took place. Second, Carol still lived there herself, so she was able to carry out the time-consuming investigation that her search required. This would not have been so easy if her birth mother had grown up in an area other than the one in which Carol was adopted, or if Carol had moved away after she grew up.

Robert will have to be a lot luckier and even more creative in order to find his birth mother. When he was approximately six weeks old, he was abandoned in a hotel in New York City. The following day, a hotel employee found him and he was turned over to the Bureau of Child Welfare. After he had lived with a foster family for a year, his foster parents formally adopted him.

Thus Robert started his search without knowing his birth date, his place of birth, his original name, or the name of his birth mother. Moreover, the agency that handled his adoption didn't have this information either. The only clue he had to go on was his adoptive mother's memory of a newspaper article about his abandonment.

After making a library search of all the newspapers then in print for the first two weeks of October the year he was abandoned, Robert finally discovered the article. In it, he found the name of the hotel, the name under which his mother had registered, and the place she listed as her hometown. Although it's possible that he now has his mother's name and his place of birth, Robert is aware his mother may have provided false information, especially if she planned to abandon him.

"What I've said all along, even when I first started thinking about searching," Robert comments, "is that I don't think I'll ever find her unless she somehow wants to be found. And up to this point, she hasn't."

Then why, in the face of such odds, does he continue to search? "It's more a matter of feeling that I have to try to locate her, rather than thinking that I can," he explains. "I wouldn't look unless I had to. Something inside me said, 'Well, if you're ever going to put these issues to rest, you need to do this.'

"It was a realization that I resisted," Robert admits. "I've pretty much had to drag myself through the entire search. It brings up a lot of questions, and I would just as soon not get into all this stuff. I do it because I have to. The alternative is not confronting these things and continuing to go through life like an emotional cripple."

Although Robert recognizes that he may never find his mother, he still has some things left to try that he feels may work. And even if he isn't successful, he's benefited from facing the painful emotions about his adoption in therapy and in his search group. "I feel as if I'm more in control over my emotions now," he states. "Before I started searching, I didn't feel my emotions were really on my side a lot of the time. I'd get angry or sad and wouldn't know why. I think I've gotten some peace of mind now. If I stopped today—which I don't plan to do—I'd say it's been worth it."

If yours was an international adoption, finding your birth mother may present some of the problems that Robert's search has. In New York City, one adoption agency alone has placed 10,000 Korean infants in the United States. Over the past decade, the number of children adopted from Latin America has also increased dramatically. Thus if you were born in another country but adopted by parents here, you—like Emily in chapter 7—have plenty of company.

Although it's certainly more difficult to search for your birth mother if she lives in another country, it's not impossible. On the positive side, many other nations do not have the same policy of sealing adoption records that we do. This means that much more information, including your mother's name, may be available to you. However, since the records of many other countries are not as systematized as ours, retrieving this information decades after the adoption may be very hard.

Whatever their particular situation, adoptees in search of their birth parents have to be as creative as possible. So, if you think a particular tactic may work, give it a try! As Emily describes in chapter 7, her adoptive mother is employed by a national network. Thus, she was able to appear on television in an effort to find her birth mother. Most adoptees do not have this opportunity, but if you get the chance to try something special, by all means, do it! As Selena's experience in chapter 7 points out, even things that seem like a very long shot sometimes actually work.

Finally, if you are refused access to important information about yourself, you have the right to petition the court to have your records made available to you. This process can become costly, and you will need to show good cause. While simply wanting to find your birth mother should be reason enough, the courts are most likely to respond if your request is based on a need for medical history.

Chapter 4

The First Contact

TRACKING down your birth mother is a difficult, frustrating, and sometimes painful process. But nothing compares to the stark terror most adoptees feel when they pick up the phone and actually call her for the first time. Adoptees all report that making the first contact can be the hardest part of the search.

They pick up the phone, dial the number, hang up, and do it again. Will she hang up on me? Will she know who I am? Will she talk to me? What if she does? What if she doesn't?

"I felt like . . . I really did feel like I was going to *die*! I thought I was going to die when I picked up that phone," Alicia remembers. "I can't even tell you what that's like!"

Although her mother acknowledged that Alicia was her daughter, the initial conversation—like many first contacts—did not go very well. "I had a very severe reaction to her, because I felt during our conversation that she was basically blowing me off and didn't want to have anything to do with me," Alicia says. "Because I think I almost expected her to react that way . . . hoping she wouldn't, but it felt like she was."

Carol's first contact with her birth mother was even more upsetting. "The first contact with her was over the phone, and she hung up on me. That was pretty devastating!

"She asked how I had gotten her number, and then said, 'You must have gotten the wrong number,' and waited," Carol continues. "At that point I was tongue-tied, and my mind was racing in so many different directions. Later on, I thought of about a hundred things I could have said, but I was just silent. She was waiting for me to say something, and when I didn't, she hung up the phone."

Fortunately, both Alicia and Carol were prepared. Because they had participated in search groups and talked to birth mothers who had already been reunited with their children, they had some idea what their mothers might have been experiencing. Remember, while you will have had months, sometimes years, to get ready emotionally for the first contact, your mother will not have had this preparation.

Unless your birth mother is searching for you and has entered her name in a registry, your call will take her completely by surprise. Thus it's important not to panic if she seems to respond badly.

At the end of their first conversation, Alicia's mother said she would call back in a week. Alicia felt that her mother was just trying to get rid of her. "But, instead, she was not blowing me off," Alicia says. "She called back three days later. We chatted, and she said, 'I was flabbergasted! How did you find me? I didn't know that was possible. They told me the records were closed.' " As it turned out, her mother's sons, who had been present when Alicia first called, do not know about her, and this had made it difficult for her mother to talk then.

Most adoptees whose first contacts did not go well agree that it was important for them to have a backup plan—first, for their own emotional sake, and second, so they could have some idea of how to continue to reach out to their birth mothers.

When Carol's mother hung up on her, "It was probably the worst three to four minutes of my life," she recalls. "I couldn't breathe or think. Once I started thinking again, and pushed those emotions down a little, I thought, 'Go on to Plan B.'

"I wrote her a short letter saying I was sorry for upsetting her but that I was sure I had the right person, and she shouldn't be afraid that I was contacting her out of anger. And I sent her a picture. She called me the night she got it!"

The First Contact

When Carol later met her, she learned what had been going through her mother's mind when Carol first called and why she hung up. "She said it was just so *unexpected!*" Carol explains. "She had never let it into her mind that something like that could happen. When she heard me on the other end of the line, she thought to herself, 'This isn't real!' She said, 'As soon as I hung up, I was kicking myself because I didn't even get a phone number!'"

Her mother also thought someone might be playing a horrible joke on her. "But then she thought about it," Carol adds, "and realized she hadn't told anyone about me." Luckily, Carol didn't give up after her initial disappointment—otherwise, two people who wanted to be reunited might never have met.

On the other hand, some birth mothers—even when they aren't prepared—react with joy when first contacted by their birth children. Laura was one of the lucky ones to get this kind of response. "She just keep saying, 'Oh, my God! Oh, my God! It's my little Debbie! Oh, my God!'" Laura recalls. Although her mother was clearly in shock, it was apparent that she was also elated to hear from Laura.

Although it's rare, occasionally adoptees do meet with real rejection when they contact their birth mother. Sharon's mother stonewalled at first, refusing to admit that she was her mother. "I kept repeating over and over, 'Is your name Teresa Mannello?' which

47

was her maiden name. And she answered, 'My name is Teresa Palma,' which is her married name. Then I repeated my birth date again and she sounded really scared. I asked her if she had a mother named June, and she hesitated, then hung up."

Sharon called back several times, but her mother said she had the wrong number. "So I wrote her a letter, and within days I got a response back. She just said that she was answering my letter because I had asked her about family medical history. Then she said, 'I don't think it's a good idea that we meet. No one in my family knows about you. They will be very upset, and I don't want to open a can of worms.' "

Her mother closed the letter with, "I hope you have a happy life, take care of your daughter, and please don't call the house, because someone might answer and I don't want to explain it was the wrong number." She also told Sharon that she looked like her when she was a baby.

Needless to say, Sharon was crushed. Still, she wrote back twice, giving her mother her new phone number. Sharon gets a lot of calls at this number that are hang-ups, and she suspects her mother may be working up the courage to call her. Anyway, that's what she hopes.

When asked if the information she received and the limited phone contact was worth the long search and ultimate rejection, Sharon replies, "Yes, at least I tried.

The First Contact

I'm happy to even have this letter from her," she adds. "How many times have I read it?"

Sharon plans to continue her efforts by writing her mother once a month, so she can let her know who she is and why she wants to meet her, and so she can convince her mother that she doesn't want to disrupt her life.

While the greatest fear of every adoptee is that they will receive the kind of rejection that Sharon has, most feel that any contact at all is better than none. Whether she accepts you or not, at least you know who your birth mother is. And you will have connected, however briefly or unsatisfactorily, with someone you are related to. For adoptees who have been rejected (and, again, this is rare), even this one contact alone has often made them feel more grounded and more at peace with themselves.

Chapter 5

Birth Mothers

ADOPTEES are not the only people who struggle with making the first contact. Birth parents like Ann who are searching for their children battle the same fear of rejection when they pick up the phone and place the initial call.

Ann's story is typical of the dilemma many unwed girls faced in the late sixties and early seventies. At nineteen, she and her boyfriend had been going together for a few years when she discovered she was pregnant. Not wanting to be "caged," her boyfriend refused to have anything to do with the situation.

Unlike him, Ann couldn't run away physically from the problem. Instead, she fled emotionally. "I was in denial," Ann recalls, "and put off telling my parents until the very last minute. I just thought, 'This can't be happening. There's no way!' So when I finally went to the doctor, I was five months pregnant and there was no turning back."

Her parents were livid. "They were basically wild, just furious!" she says. "I had always been a *very* good girl—not even drinking. I had never done anything wrong."

Her parents were also grief stricken. "I swore I would never do anything to make my father cry, and when he found out I was pregnant, he cried. So, I thought, 'Oh, my God! I have *really* done something terrible!' From the time I discovered I was pregnant, I just went into a state of shame. I would have done anything to make that right for them again.

"I also knew that if you didn't get married, the only thing that was done then was that you surrendered the child for adoption," Ann continues. The family's minister also strongly encouraged this, and Ann's father, who bowed to authority figures, was swayed by his advice. Ann's mother, on the other hand, had reservations about this decision but believed that adoption was what Ann wanted.

Ann's attempt to protect her boyfriend only made things worse. "My parents never really liked him, so I refused to tell them who the father was," Ann remembers. "I told them I got drunk one night and had sex with someone I just met once." Unfortunately, that made it easier for her parents to believe that Ann might not want to keep the child. "So, I sabotaged myself without knowing it," she adds, sadly.

Ann was placed in a home for unwed mothers in another city, where no one would recognize her. The agency staff advised her parents not to become involved in Ann's decision about the baby's future. "What they told my parents was to stay out of it, that it was my life and they shouldn't express any feelings pro or con, so that I could make up my own mind." Her parents had previously planned a vacation, and the agency recommended that they go ahead and take it.

Cut off from her parents, Ann was subjected to unrelenting pressure from the agency. "There were daily therapy sessions with a social worker who would get you to make lists of what you could offer your baby and what someone else could. It wasn't why you should keep it and why you shouldn't, it was what can you give him," she says.

"They also stressed over and over how very selfish I was to think of keeping my baby, that I wasn't thinking about my baby, I was only thinking of myself. 'If you really love your baby, you'll give him to two people who can raise him properly and give him all the things that he'll need in life,' they said. This came to me day after day," Ann recalls bitterly.

Ann delivered her baby, a son, while her parents were still on vacation. Although she was aware that she couldn't keep him, Ann demanded to be allowed to feed him like the other mothers in the hospital. "They brought me my son every feeding time," she says. "I had to have him with me because I knew that was the only time I was going to have with him. And I told him over and over, 'I'll see you again when you're a teenager.' "

In spite of the pressure to surrender her son, Ann resisted in the only way she knew how. "Even after I went home, I refused for a month and a half to sign the papers. The baby was in foster care, I presume with his adoptive parents. Nobody told me I could have seen him at the time.

"I argued with my parents gently," she continues. "I showed them the pictures and told them I wanted to keep him." But Ann was unable to change their minds. "Finally, I just couldn't fight any more," she says.

According to Ann, her search for her son, Andrew, started "the minute he left my arms." She says, "I had pulled together a lot of the pieces of where he might be by the time he was five, but I couldn't act on it then." The feelings it stirred up were just too painful.

Years went by. "I was friends with an adoptee since childhood, and I had helped her search for her birth parents, and even with all that I couldn't touch it. Finally, she invited me to go on a march on Washington sponsored by adoptees and birth parents, and I decided to go for it. I made a big sign that said, 'This birth mother wants to be found!' on one side and put a picture of Andrew and his birth date and the hospital he was born in on the other."

As it happened, a woman who lived near that hospital approached Ann and introduced her to a person skilled in finding adoptees. With the help of the nonidentifying information Ann had received from the agency and other facts Ann had been able to uncover from friends of her family's minister, the man was able to locate Andrew within a week.

Once she knew Andrew's adopted name and telephone number, she told her family. "When my brother heard the name, he just looked at me in disbelief and said, 'No! Get out of here!' " Ann says. By a strange coincidence, her brother was an assistant manager in a music store where Andrew had worked three years earlier!

By the time Ann found her son, Andrew had just turned twenty-one. After careful rehearsal, Ann finally placed the initial call. "I said, 'I don't want to upset you, but I have reason to believe because of the research that I've done that I'm your birth mother.' " Unfortunately, Andrew's response was not what she'd hoped for. "There was just dead silence at the end of the phone," she says.

Nervously, Ann stressed that he didn't have to have contact with her, but it was important to her that he know she had always wanted to find him, and she was there for him. She ended by saying she just needed to know if he was alive and well.

After what seemed like forever, Andrew finally spoke. "I'm very well adjusted to being adopted, and I have no ill will against anyone involved. I'm sure you did what you felt you had to do," he said. Ann responded by saying that she was sure he must be in shock and probably needed some time to think about all this. She also asked if he wanted to write down her name and address. To her relief, he said yes.

When a month had passed and Ann heard nothing from him, she wrote him a long, very emotional letter. "It obviously overwhelmed him," she admits. As she later learned, her son began to fear things would escalate and she'd end up on his doorstep. Two weeks after she sent the letter, Ann received a reply from his lawyer stating that Andrew didn't want her to correspond with him. However, if she moved, the lawyer requested that she leave a forwarding address with the adoption agency in case he changed his mind at a later date.

"I was completely bewildered, completely devastated!" Ann says. "I blamed his adoptive parents— which probably wasn't fair. But if I wasn't angry at them, then I'd have to be angry at him. And I couldn't afford that."

It has now been three years since Ann spoke to Andrew, and he hasn't contacted her. She wrote him a few letters during this period, but when he graduated from college, she lost track of his whereabouts.

Ann's painful experience provides some insight into why birth mothers may react negatively when first contacted by their children. The possibility of losing their child a second time is just too frightening. "When you unfold yourself that much that you're willing to open up and meet them, and then the person walks out, it's just more than most people can manage," Ann explains. "Which is why I think that some birth mothers refuse to meet initially."

Although Beth's experience as a twenty-year-old, pregnant, unwed college student was similar to Ann's, the outcome of her reunion with her son couldn't have been more different. While on spring break in Italy, Beth spent a few days touring with a student from Brazil. Although they had sex only once, Beth sensed immediately that she was pregnant. Because of this, "The next day, I took his picture and made him write his full name in my address book," she says.

Beth's suspicions were correct. "I left Europe pregnant, came home, and kept my secret," she says. "He came through the States on his way home, looked me up, and I went to a party with him."

While at the party, she tried to take him aside to talk, but with no success. "A guest found me in the bedroom crying and asked what was the matter," Beth recalls. "I said I needed to speak to Alberto alone and asked if he would go get him. Alberto wouldn't come, and the young man asked if he could give him a message. I said, 'Would you tell him I'm pregnant.' "

He returned with Alberto's response—"You can't prove it's my baby, and anyway, it's your problem." Beth asked the young man to walk her to the subway, and she went home.

"I knew I was on my own then," she says. "I never saw him again, never heard from him again, nothing."

Beth's parents responded to the news of her pregnancy in much the same way as Ann's—they were furious. Without a husband, there was no question of her keeping the child. Like Ann, Beth was sent away. She went to work as a nanny for a family selected by Catholic Charities. "We were driving up to the house, and my mother was berating me the whole way up in the car," Beth remembers. "Finally, I said to her, 'Mom, I'm not a bad girl.' And she whipped her head around and said, 'Good girls don't have bastard babies!'

"I was very protective of my baby," Beth continues, "and I refused to let anyone call him names, my mother of all people!" Her mother's reaction was so rejecting that it permanently alienated Beth.

"More than anything, I wanted to be welcomed back into my family," Beth explains. "I did what I had to do so that my family wouldn't be angry at me forever.

I didn't want to be a leper anymore, I wanted to be loved again. There weren't any alternatives!"

The pain of surrendering her son felt as though it would kill her, however. "I thought I'd die when I had to hand him over to the nurse. When they say 'heartbreaking,' I never knew it could be literal!"

After ten years Beth married, and she helped raise her husband's three children from his previous marriage. She had told her husband about her son on their second date, but she never believed she would see the child again. "I was told repeatedly, and I really believed, that the records were sealed. I had heard vague noises about reunions, but I always thought it must have been private adoptions where the lawyers knew who the people were and gave them the names. I thought cases like mine were hopeless, impossible."

When her son was seventeen, Beth read about Soundex Registry in the newspaper and sent away for an application. The form asked for detailed data. Beth had no problem with her name and address, the baby's name, and the baby's birth date, but when it came to the name of the hospital, she couldn't remember. Nor could Beth remember the city in which he had been born.

Although many birth mothers are so traumatized that they recall *nothing* about their child's birth, Beth didn't know that this type of amnesia was common. Thus, she assumed her inability to remember meant she didn't care. "I thought that was the only reason I could have forgotten," she says.

"So, I never sent the form in because I was too ashamed. I thought it showed that I was really superficial and unloving, and that all the things they said about 'bad women' must have been true. I knew I cared," Beth adds, "but it didn't make sense that if I did, I could forget." That was the end of her effort to search.

Her son, however, had been determined to know his origins since childhood, and when he turned twenty-one, he started actively searching. Three years later, Beth got the surprise of her life. The phone rang and when she answered, a man asked her if it was a good time for her to talk and whether he could ask her a few questions. "I thought, 'Great, it's some poll,' " Beth recalls. The caller asked her if her maiden name was Beth Martin, and if her father was Jim Martin of Bedford Business School.

"My father is seventy-six and he has a heart condition," Beth continues, "so when he asked if Jim Martin was my father, I thought he was an intern from the hospital calling the next of kin. My heart stopped! I got very officious and said, 'Look, if there's a problem, please identify yourself and tell me what this is all about, or this conversation will terminate.'

"And he said, 'Oh, please! Don't hang up! I've been looking for you for three years. I think I'm your biological son.'

Where Are My Birth Parents?

"I just stopped," Beth recalls. "He said 'biological son,' and at first it didn't mean anything. I was confused for a minute. Then 'son' came through, and I saw stars in front of my eyes. I sat down very quickly on my bed, and asked, 'Are you Timmy?' He said that Timothy had been his birth name, but now his name was Donald.

"It was like being told that you won the lottery," Beth says, trying to describe her feelings at this point. "As if you had a son who you thought was missing in action, and for all those years, you thought he might be in some dreadful tiger cage somewhere awful. And then you find out that he actually bailed out over a tropical island with coconuts and palm trees and dancing girls, and he was fine! And all these years, you didn't know!"

Donald had been particularly lucky in his search. Somehow his adoptive parents not only knew Beth's last name but had remembered it. Since this is probably the most difficult piece of information to uncover, Donald started his search ahead of the game. He was also told Beth's father had been a school principal and that she had gone to a Catholic college. With this information and a lot of work, he was able to find Beth. Donald's adoptive parents were supportive of his search, and his mother had even helped by making a crucial phone call for information.

Within a week of their first conversation, Donald visited Beth and her family. The two had no problems establishing a relationship and spent the next four days talking, crying, looking at photo albums, and getting to know each other.

They then decided to try to find Donald's father, Alberto. Because Beth had carefully saved the address book from her trip to Europe, they knew his full name. In a truly Herculean effort, Beth was able to determine that there was *no one* with Alberto's last name in all of Brazil, the country she thought he was from. She then went through over 300 phone books from cities in Europe and Latin America. Finally, she did a computer search of everyone in the United States with his surname—a grand total of eleven individuals. Ten of these people were related, and all knew of each other, but none had ever heard of Alberto. Neither were they acquainted with the eleventh person, a woman in Florida.

Beth wrote two letters to her in English that went unanswered. Finally she sent her a third letter written in Portuguese. In it she included a questionnaire asking whether she knew Alberto and, if so, where he was; where her family came from; and if she would be willing to forward a letter to Alberto on her behalf.

This time the woman responded, telling her that her family was originally from Ecuador. Moreover, she said she had already forwarded the two previous letters to Alberto—and if he hadn't answered, it wasn't her fault.

Luckily, Ecuador has a relatively small population. By checking copies of the phone directories, Beth was able to locate Alberto's address. Donald immediately sent his father a letter, enclosing Beth's photograph of Alberto from the sixties and a current picture of himself. Since Donald was the spitting image of Alberto, both Beth and he knew Alberto would have no doubt that he was his son.

Alberto had clearly grown up since the day he told Beth that her pregnancy was her problem. Now in his second marriage and the father of four children, he and his wife called the day they received Donald's letter. As it turned out, Alberto's wife is American and the couple frequently comes to the United States, so Donald will soon meet his father too.

The only problem Beth and Donald have encountered is the reaction of Donald's adoptive parents to their ongoing relationship. When they thought that Donald was interested only in connecting with his roots and becoming grounded, they were quite comfortable with their son's effort to find Beth and had even provided assistance. What they had not counted on was that Beth and Donald might become close. Donald's adoptive mother in particular has been quite threatened by this development, although recently things seem to be easing up in that regard.

Interestingly, Beth joined a search group *after* her son found her, initially to get help in searching for Alberto.

But she found that the group has been useful in giving her a place to sort out her feelings and to manage her new relationship with Donald. Ann is part of a search group too. She gains enormous support from adoptees and other birth mothers in dealing with the pain of her son's rejection. Conversely, the insights and experiences of women like Beth and Ann help adoptees understand some of the reasons birth mothers surrender their infants, how surrender affects mothers, and what they might expect when they first contact their own birth mothers.

Ann's and Beth's experiences also illustrate a number of important points. First, not all adoptees feel a need to search, and some may not even wish to be found. On the other hand, many birth parents who don't search may desperately long for a reunion. Finally, birth parents who search face the very same terrifying fear of rejection that adoptees do. Like them, these parents usually decide the risk is worth it.

Chapter 6

Reunion and Postreunion

Y OU found her! You spoke to your birth mother on the phone, and like most birth mothers who have been contacted by their children, she hasn't rejected you. Now you're going to meet each other! Or, if you haven't gotten that far yet, at least you and she have decided to talk further or to correspond. In any event, it looks as if you may have the opportunity to have a relationship with her.

But what does this mean? If you're like most adoptees, you're probably not sure exactly what kind of relationship you want, to say nothing of what she may expect. You know that being reunited with your birth mother will affect your life, but you aren't at all sure how. As many adoptees who have been through this before will tell you, "Expect the unexpected!"

Some aspects of your reunion will probably be wonderful. Because adoptees have had so few facts about their origins—and so many fantasies—sometimes their lives haven't seemed completely real. Thus for many adoptees, merely having made the initial contact with their birth mothers, regardless of how well the meeting went, gives them a sense of reality about their lives that had been missing. This alone can be worth the entire search, even when the relationship with your birth mother turns out to be less than what you'd hoped.

After a lifetime of looking different from everyone else in your family, recognizing features on your birth mother's face that resemble your own can be a thrilling experience. Even if you and your birth mother don't look anything alike, you may find that aspects of your personalities are very similar. If, like most adoptees, you grew up not knowing anyone you were genetically related to, learning which parts of yourself you've inherited from another person can be very exciting.

Another extremely important, but scarier, aspect of the reunion is the opportunity to finally have your questions answered. "Why did you give me up?" and "Did you love me?" are the two questions every adoptee wants to ask. Getting to hear from your mother herself why she surrendered you and how she felt about having to make this choice will help you deal with your own feelings about being abandoned and feeling unlovable.

For teenage adoptees, who have grown up at a time when unmarried women feel free to keep their children, understanding the stigma and social pressures their mothers faced in the early and mid-seventies can be hard. Those of you who join a search group will probably meet birth mothers who can describe to you what being unwed and pregnant during this period was like, but this is not the same as having your own mother explain why *she* felt she had to surrender you.

As to whether or not your birth mother loved you, only she truly knows. Thus, no matter how much others may try to reassure you that she did, she is the only one on earth who can convincingly answer this question for you.

Although you and your birth mother may both have wanted to be reunited very much, getting to know each other is not going to be easy for either of you. It's important to accept that this will be a very confusing time, and that each of you may experience emotions you never expected. After all, there is no precedent for establishing this kind of relationship, and nothing either of you has experienced in life has prepared you to deal with a situation like this.

One thing that neither you nor your birth mother may expect is that when you are reunited, both of you are likely to regress emotionally to the time when you were surrendered. When a mother and child are abruptly separated, the nurturing process is short-circuited for both of them. At reunions, the process often resumes on a psychological level, but this time neither the age nor the circumstance of the mother and child are appropriate.

Thus your mother may try to go back and give you the nurturing she was unable to give you before. But the nurturing she has in mind is the kind one gives to an infant, not to an adolescent or an adult. On the one hand, this can be very irritating to you as her teenage child. But at the same time, you may find that deep in your heart, being nurtured like an infant is exactly what you want. Obviously, these conflicting feelings can be very confusing!

No matter how much you may want it, however, to be nurtured as an infant when you are now a teenager or adult is not the same as having had that nurturing when you were a baby. The sense that their birth mothers' nurturing is too little and too late often makes adoptees very angry and very sad. Handling these emotions is especially difficult because most adoptees don't understand them.

Of all the emotions you are likely to experience, anger and rage are the hardest to deal with, in part because most adoptees don't want to admit they have these feelings. Not only is it painful and frightening to feel this angry, but adoptees often worry that their rage will get out of control and disrupt the relationship they are trying to build with their birth mother. Unfortunately, no matter what you find at the end of your search, some part of it is guaranteed to make you tremendously angry.

Sometimes, as in Laura's case, what you wanted most to find is what makes you the angriest. Some adoptees hope that their birth parents eventually married, because this would be an indication that their mother and father truly cared about each other and proof that, as the product of this couple, they were born out of love. Others worry that their birth may have ruined their mother's life. Laura felt both these things.

In her initial telephone conversation with her birth mother, Laura learned that a few years after her birth, her parents had married and now had two sons, Laura's full brothers. From the way her mother spoke, Laura could tell that she had a close family and a happy life. Laura was elated and relieved to hear this—at first.

When she got to meet her in person, Laura liked her mother even more. But, to her surprise, the fact that her mother was so great made her furious. "She was the nicest woman I could have met," Laura says. "I couldn't want anybody nicer—damn her!"

In her search group, Laura had heard many others talk about being angry at their birth mothers, but this just wasn't something she thought she would feel herself. "As much as I thought I was prepared, I was really totally unprepared for how I was going to feel," she recalls. "Because up until the minute I met her, I never felt anything but real positive feelings. I never tapped into any of the anger and resentment that people talk about."

Her mother had brought pictures of Laura's father and brothers for her to see. "I think she may have been over-killing to make me realize that I was a product of love, but after a couple of hours of looking at pictures of this obviously really *happy*, close family, what happened with me was the feeling, 'Well, I'm glad you have your happy little family, but there's one family member missing from all these family pictures!' "

Both Laura and her mother had wanted a chance to get to know each other before introducing Laura to the rest of the family. But shortly after their initial meeting, Laura met her father and brothers. She likes them all a lot too. Far from ruining her mother's life, as Laura came to understand, giving her up for adoption was what made it possible for her mother to go on to have a wonderful marriage and family. "I know if they had kept me at seventeen, chances are that marriage would not have worked then. They wouldn't have been joining together for the right reasons. It would have been out of necessity," Laura says.

"They were allowed to finish their adolescence, and then when they were ready, they went on and got married. And that angered me in a way, because I feel like their giving me up is what enabled them to have their happy life."

Laura's feelings are complicated by the fact that

the family that adopted her was not a happy one, something she hadn't told her birth mother. "And what she [her birth mother] doesn't know, because I haven't really bothered to paint any other picture, is that I came from a *very* unhappy family. And I guess the anger was kind of like, 'Wow, look at this happy family, and what about me? I end up in this family that hates each other and is miserable together, and I'm glad you are all having such a good time!'" Thus, in a very real sense, Laura feels that her birth parents' happiness was purchased at her expense, and naturally this makes her both angry and sad.

Has finding all this out been worth the pain to Laura? "I'm really glad that I know, but part of that is wrapped up in the fact that I found normal, decent parents," she answers. "For me, that's a good part of it. I know that they're not mentally ill, that they're not psychopaths, that they're not criminals, they're really *nice* people. And that makes me *very, very* happy!"

It's also helped her feel comfortable about the heritage she has to offer her two-year-old son, who will know both Laura's and her husband's families. "It makes me feel good, because I'm raising my child, and I know where his people are and what he comes from, and that's important to me.

"I'm also glad because it gives me a better sense of who I am," Laura adds. "I can't really say that I know [my birth parents] well yet, but what I know of them,

I'm very proud to be a part of them, because I think they're really good people. I'm glad of that. . . . I'm glad to know who I'm from and what I'm about!"

Particularly in the early postreunion stage, you and your birth mother may have real difficulty in comprehending where the other is coming from and what each of you is really feeling. Considering that the two of you don't know each other, this is hardly surprising, but it can be very painful and confusing.

Alicia's birth mother has been willing to talk with her over the phone, but she certainly hasn't opened up to her the way Alicia had hoped. She answers Alicia's questions but doesn't volunteer information or seem to want to know much about Alicia. When Alicia asked her for a photograph, she avoided the issue, and she hasn't asked Alicia for a picture in return.

Although her birth mother's husband knows about Alicia, the couple's two sons do not. Since her mother feels "the timing isn't right" to tell them about Alicia, she can't talk freely when Alicia calls if one of the sons is in the house. While Alicia tries to understand her mother's position, the fact that her mother hides her existence from her sons makes Alicia feel like a dirty secret.

Thus Alicia was completely taken off guard when, at the end of a conversation, her mother said, "I love you." "It hit me like a ton of bricks," Alicia recalls, "because I wasn't expecting it. And yet there was this initial reaction of me wanting to say, 'I love you too.' And yet also saying, 'I don't *know* you!' But I do know her . . . That was a moment very fraught with, 'Oh, my God! I'm confused! What is this relationship?' "

Although Alicia is disappointed with her mother's response to her, she—like Laura—feels her search has been worth it. For one thing, she learned how much her mother had wanted to keep her, and this information has meant a lot.

"My mother said, 'I didn't see you in the hospital. Alicia, if I'd held you in the hospital, I wouldn't have let go. I *have* to let you know, it was the most difficult decision I ever had to make in my entire life. I did *not* want to give you up for adoption. I went to your father and he completely denied all responsibility. In those days, it was not acceptable for a single woman to be a mother.' "

Just as the open and loving reception Laura received from her birth parents has had its pain, Alicia's less-than-hoped-for relationship with her birth mother has had an up side, at least for her. Alicia is especially close to her adoptive parents. In spite of the fact that she reassures them of her love, she knows they still worry that somehow her birth mother may replace them in her heart.

"I think in the long run, it's helped me that it [her relationship with her birth mother] hasn't been a fairy-tale relationship," Alicia says. "Maybe this is an excuse, but I think in some ways it seems less threatening to my parents, particularly my mother. And I've always been very, very protective of her."

As you and your birth mother struggle to get to know each other, there may be a lot of testing on both sides. You may look for reassurance that your birth mother isn't going to abandon you again, while she may test you to see if you are going to try to get even for the abandonment.

Both of you will have to grapple with the problem of what kind of relationship you want to have with each other. Adoptees often feel pulled back and forth by conflicting needs for closeness and distance. "I love you, I hate you, I'm smarter than you, I don't like your clothes, I need you, I don't want you"—you may have all of these feelings in the space of a day. Crazy as this can make both you and your birth mother feel, these emotions are all normal under the circumstance.

What should you call your birth mother? Does she want you to call her Mom? Do you want to call her Mom? How will your adoptive mother feel if you call your birth mother Mom? How will your birth mother's other children feel if you, a stranger, call their mother Mom?

Both you and your birth mother may have loyalties to other people that can influence how free you feel to become involved in each other's lives. Carol's birth mother has a younger daughter, Denise, who is not happy about Carol's sudden appearance in their lives.

Although Carol's birth mother would like to establish a closer relationship with her, she doesn't want to upset her other daughter. "She and Denise are in this very close relationship," Carol says. "I think my mother feels that as long as Denise has not accepted my existence, she isn't going to make a lot of overt moves toward me."

While Alicia and Carol's birth mothers are concerned about how their other children will respond to the adoptee and to their mother's hidden past, adoptees like Alicia often worry that the relationship with their birth mother will make their adoptive parents feel abandoned. Being able to step back and put yourself in the other person's shoes can really be helpful in dealing with these problems. Both you and your birth mother will need to give each other a lot of latitude for a considerable period of time—a year to eighteen months perhaps—while you adjust to each other.

The expectations you have are among the most important determinants of how successful you will be in relating to your birth parents. Some adoptees believe that finding their birth mother will change their lives and make everything better. This can be especially true if you are a teenager in the middle of the "my parents are the stupidest people in the world" stage. At this age, it can be very easy to imagine that your "real" parents would never make the mistakes you feel your adoptive parents have made.

Reunion and Postreunion

At the other extreme are those who think that finding their birth mother won't be that big a thing, that it's just curiosity that prompts their search, and that she'll be just a friend. But your birth mother can't really be your friend, because she's your mother. And no matter how casually you approach your search, finding your birth mother will be a powerful emotional experience.

The adoptees who handle their reunion best are those who can let go of their expectations and let the relationship grow naturally. Keep in mind that each of you has had your own life for the period of separation. There may be a lot of similarities and differences between you in style, personality, and culture. Sometimes these things will blend easily and sometimes they won't. What you can hope to establish with your birth mother is a caring relationship as an adult with an older adult who happens to be your mother. It's not easy, but the rewards are well worth the effort.

Finally, it's important to understand that being reunited with your birth mother won't change the fact that you're adopted. A reunion never takes away the pain and hurt of adoption. A reunion, however, may make it easier to deal with your feelings about your life.

Chapter 7

Firsthand Experience: Chloe, Emily, and Selena

WHAT is it like to be a teenager searching for your birth parents? As the stories of these three young women illustrate, the experience can vary widely.

Chloe is in the middle of her search. She has discovered her birth parents' names. Now all she has to do is to locate them—something she is confident will happen in the next few months.

So far, Emily's search has been less successful. Since hers was an international adoption, her task has been much harder. Although she hasn't given up hope, she now faces the possibility that she may never find her birth mother. Nevertheless, in the process of searching, she's learned much about herself—including her real name—and has had a chance to experience her native culture firsthand. Most important, she knows she gave it her best shot.

Firsthand Experience

Finally, Selena has successfully located her birth mother—who was delighted to be found—and is now slowly building a relationship with her.

CHLOE

The day she learned she was adopted still sticks in Chloe's mind. "I remember this so clearly, which is pretty amazing because it was nursery school," she says. "But they read a book about a little boy who'd gotten adopted. I didn't understand what the story was about, so I ran home and asked my mother."

Her mother took her to the library, where she read the book to Chloe. "I asked her if I was adopted. And she said yes. I was really confused! I was so little, it was like, 'Why am I here? You're not my mom.' "

Although Chloe became adjusted to the idea that she was adopted, she experienced the same sense of not being grounded, of not knowning who she was, that many adoptees do. "You wake up in the morning, you walk down the street to get a paper or something. And there's someone who looks sort of like you, and immediately, that light turns on. 'Hmm, I wonder . . .' You don't go a day without wondering who you are talking to," she tries to explain.

"Or you get up in the morning and you look in the mirror. Everybody—I'm talking about the normal, everyday nonadoptee—sees somebody and thinks, 'My

God, I look like my father,' or 'More and more, I'm beginning to look like my mother.' An adoptee looks in the mirror and they can't see anything, because they don't have anything to put that up against. You don't truly see your face, because you can't put it up against anything else," she continues.

The feeling of looking like no one she knew was accentuated by the fact that Chloe's appearance is very different from others in her family. "My sister [who was born to her parents after Chloe was adopted] and my mother are very buxom. I'm not—at all!" she says. "They have different skin coloring. I'm the only blond-haired person in my family. My father's only five feet seven, my mother's five five, and my sister's five feet. And I'm five ten! I stick out like a sore thumb."

Unfortunately, Chloe looked different not only from family members but from the vast majority of her family's ethnic group. "I went to Hebrew high school, and there was a time in my life when I was very religious. I was the most religious in my family, actually." But looking ethnically "wrong" made the connection with her religion difficult.

"It's hard going into a temple and everybody looks somehow Jewish. I look *nothing* like that. It's very rare that you're going to find a tall, blond, green-eyed, pointy-nose girl walking into a temple," Chloe says. "I always get double looks when I walk into my temple.

Firsthand Experience

And then it's like, 'Oh yeah, that's Richard and Joan Stein's daughter.' "

For Chloe, searching for her birth mother has been something she wanted to do for as long as she can remember. Her parents had always said they would help her if she ever wanted them to, but Chloe suspected that they may have made the offer never thinking they would have to follow through.

After years of wanting to search, her decision to actually begin looking for her birth mother was triggered by a very ordinary event when she was in her late teens. "I'm an actress, and I was doing a film," she explains. "And I was on my way to be filmed for the first scene. And this woman walked down the street who had nothing to do with anything—she was just a woman walking down the street. But she looked very much like me.

"And for some reason—I mean, it was no big deal, I get that every day—but for some reason, I couldn't get it out of my head the whole night. I kept thinking, 'Forget it, I can't handle not knowing this kind of stuff.' "

Chloe had seen a television program about a search group in her town but was afraid to make the call herself. "I have to be perfectly honest with you," she admits. "I was horrified to call, so a friend called for me."

Like many adoptees, the idea of actually searching stirred up a lot of questions and feelings for Chloe.

79

"They sent me information, and I had it sitting in my room for about a year and a half," she recalls. "I was questioning. I was afraid, and I had also read some books and stuff about how the government was pushing it away, and I thought, 'There's no way I'm ever going to get anywhere!'

"I also thought I wasn't old enough 'cause kids who are adopted, they're like, 'Don't you have to be twenty-one to do that?' And when I was fifteen, that's what I thought. *And I could have done it!*" she adds with chagrin.

Joining the search group helped her deal with her anger toward her birth mother and to understand what her adoptive parents would probably experience during her search. "Before I started going to the meetings, there was some anger toward my birth mother," Chloe recalls.

"Because, as far as I knew, she was some woman who fit the stereotypical drunken teenager, you know. This is the way I looked at it—slime, dirt of the earth, scum on your shoes, everything. I imagined that this young girl, probably drugged up, probably slimy and disgusting, screwed up, had me, and decided she couldn't hold the responsibility and turned me out the door."

There were several birth mothers in her search group, however, something that proved very helpful to her in dealing with this anger—not that she had any interest in meeting them at the time. "Let me tell you," she says, "the first day I saw a birth mother in there, I was going to kill someone! I was like, 'What are you doing here?' But the truth of the matter is most birth mothers didn't have a choice. I realize that now."

The group has continued to be a godsend for Chloe. "I'm learning so much even now, and I've been going there for a while. I'm learning what my birth parents are probably feeling, I'm learning more about myself than I ever knew. I think those are all important, because if I didn't know all that, I'd really be putting myself in a bind. I wouldn't know what to say [to my birth mother], and the reunion would probably stink!"

It's not always easy to go to meetings, however. "Every time I go, I've had a normal day, everything was fine, I think to myself, 'All right, this is going to be fine. Nothing's going to happen,' " Chloe says. "And I always leave in tears. Always! It hasn't failed me yet!

"There's so much emotion bottled up," she explains. "It's fear, it's anxiety, it's not knowing who you are, it's not knowing where you come from. For most adoptees, they don't even know if their birth certificate is a fact. You don't know your real name. You're just a walking *nothing* as far as I'm concerned. It's horrible! But that's the way it is."

Chloe has used what she's learned in the group to approach her parents. "I kind of sat them down when I really started doing it, and I said, 'Look, you know, I

81

think it's important that we do this together as a family, because [otherwise] you're going to feel that rejection.' Because there is a feeling of rejection. But if I do it with them, when there's still that bond of parent and child, it's not like I'm going off to find my other mother."

Her parents go through periods of feeling threatened, but Chloe expects that and knows it's natural. "Recently, when I started getting all the information, they've been getting *really, really* scared," she says.

Her mother and father handle their anxiety differently, though. "You know, my dad doesn't really want to know about it. Of course, if I ever got really upset or if it happened, he wouldn't just shut off. He would be there."

But he doesn't really understand why Chloe needs to search. As Chloe says, "Of course, I want to know who I am and where I come from, just the basic questions of life that everybody else gets to know. And he doesn't see why it's important for me to know if I have that with our family.

"My mother, on the other hand, is slowly getting a grasp on it," Chloe says. She wants to know everything that's happening with the search. "She calls me up every day and says, 'Anything new? Anything new?' She said to me, 'I wouldn't be able to go and meet this other person. But if you ever needed a shoulder to cry on or somebody to hold your hand, whatever, I'll always be there.' She's wonderful!"

Firsthand Experience

Her mother's reaction has been a bit of a surprise to Chloe. "It's strange, but I'd never really gotten along with my mother until this year when I started searching. It's bringing us closer," she says. Although neither Chloe nor her mother had anticipated this, it's something that frequently happens when adoptive parents help their children search.

Although she has been searching for a relatively short time, Chloe got an unusual break. She found out her birth name and birth parents' names before she got her nonidentifying information.

"People can struggle for this for years, and I had this piece of paper sitting in the room, which I didn't think meant anything," she remembers. The paper was from a search group in Texas, where Chloe was born. The group acts on behalf of adoptees in petitioning the court to unseal their records.

"It was on my desk for about six months. I was told it was going to take about a hundred times before this sort of thing would work, so that's why I neglected even doing it in the first place," Chloe explains. Finally, she mailed it in.

Evidently, the search group knew a judge that was sympathetic to requests from adoptees. "Three days later, I get a Federal Express package at my door with all my information," she continues. "I mean, that doesn't happen!"

At first, Chloe was too overwhelmed even to open

the package. "For some reason, I knew what was in there," she recalls. "I couldn't walk, I couldn't talk, I couldn't swallow. I put the envelope down on my desk. I didn't even open it. I just sat on my bed and stared at it."

Her mother happened to call at this point. Excitedly, she urged Chloe to open the package. "Finally, I opened it up, and it was my birth mother's name, my name, everything!"

Chloe has written the Bureau of Vital Statistics in Texas and expects to get her nonidentifiying information soon. "That will fill me in on a lot of information about myself," she adds. These facts plus the identifying information she received should enable her to locate both her birth parents, something she expects to happen soon.

Where does she go from here? What does she hope from a reunion with her birth mother? "I'm ready to handle anything now," Chloe declares. "If she wants to reject me—and there's only a five percent chance of that—then, by all means, just let me see her once. Send me a picture. I just want that connection that I should have had at least once in my life, and that I never had.

"I want her to be comfortable," she adds. "I want her to know that I'm not her enemy. That if she ever needs somebody, I'm *there*. She rejected me, but I'm fine with that now. You know what I mean? She put me into the world at the same time."

Chloe would like, if possible, to have a relationship with her birth mother. "I don't think I'd ever call her Mom, though," she adds. "These [her adoptive parents] are my parents, they brought me up. They did their parenting. That's what a parent does. This woman also put me into the world, so I've got to be grateful about that.

"And when I do meet her, I'll just show up with a bunch of flowers—'cause I do love her, whoever she is."

EMILY

In several important respects, Emily's experience has been different from that of Chloe and Selena. First, Emily was adopted not as an infant but as a child of almost three. Second, Emily was born in Korea, so hers was an international adoption. Third, her parents did not adopt because they were unable to have children. They already had a son of their own, although at only two years of age, he was younger than Emily.

Emily describes her parents' reasons for adopting her: "They had a child, they had my brother. And they wanted to adopt someone else who was less fortunate, so they wanted to adopt an overseas child."

Because of postwar conditions, there were plenty of Korean children in need of homes. As Emily describes it, "After the war and for years and years after, people fell apart, their lives, their businesses, or whatever. It was at the point where to raise a child was almost impossible. If you had five children, there was no way you could raise a sixth. Some people lost their children, or abandoned their children, or someone took their children away. It was just horrible!"

As can happen with a child her age, Emily lost conscious memory of her previous life and didn't realize her adoptive parents were not her original family. It wasn't until she started school that she was even aware that she looked different from the rest of her family. Her peers soon let her know, however.

"Growing up with my brother, Jason, we played a lot. And when we got to school, all the children said, 'You don't look like your brother.' And I said, 'Yes, I do.'" But when they persisted in pointing out the difference, Emily went home and asked her mother why the other children said she and Jason didn't look alike.

"And she told me, 'That's because you're adopted.'" For a child who hadn't realized she was different, being adopted suddenly meant she didn't look like the rest of her family.

Although her teachers treated her like the other children, the kids in her class did not. "I don't think it was because I was adopted," she says. "But I definitely think it was because I was Korean. There were very few Asians in my school."

Firsthand Experience

Like Chloe, Emily had difficulty fitting into the ethnic culture of her adoptive family. "Everyone tells me I'm Jewish, but I'm in this little Korean body. If I was in Korea, I'd either be Christian or Buddhist, but certainly not Jewish."

On the other hand, Emily had no interest in finding her birth parents—she was just too angry at them. "For a long time, I didn't want to search," she says. "At school, everybody used to ask me if I ever wanted to find my mom. I said *no!* with the most resentment possible. I had so much anger that she had left me.

"I always thought, 'Oh, I'm happy here,' even though my family wasn't that great. My parents got divorced, my mom was changing jobs a lot, so it wasn't that good. And my mom and I used to fight almost daily."

Emily's adoptive status had a lot to do with these fights, although she never suspected that until she and her mother sought help from a psychotherapist—a man who was also an adoptee—for help in improving their relationship. "I always felt like I was the bad kid because I fought with her," Emily recalls. "My brother was always smarter than me, and he got along better with my parents, so I always thought I was the black sheep of the family. It was good to find out that a lot of these feelings were because I was adopted—that it was normal, that I wasn't such a freak, or whatever," she continues.

She also began to realize why she never felt happy on her birthday. For many adoptees, this day is also the time when they were surrendered for adoption—hardly a cause for celebration. But Emily has another reason for being depressed on her supposed birthday. It's another reminder of all the things she doesn't know about herself.

"I can't really say, 'Oh, February nineteeth, it's my birthday.' This year, it really hit me hard. I realized how *morbid* the day was for me. It isn't my birthday! It was made up! It's a day I shouldn't even celebrate." Because she was abandoned at a police station in Korea, her exact birth date is unknown. But since she was old enough to speak at the time and knew her name, that part of her records proved to be accurate.

Before she sought professional help, Emily had never been able to talk to her parents about her feelings about her birthday, about not knowing anything about herself, or about adoption itself. "When I was growing up, I wouldn't have thought about talking to them about this 'cause it hurt me too much. I was afraid they were going to reject me. I couldn't deal with being rejected by two families!"

With the help of a therapist, Emily was able to begin to deal with her feelings about being adopted, emotions that she had tried to ignore for years. And she decided she wanted to find her birth mother and connect with her culture and family heritage.

Firsthand Experience

"It's not an obsession, it's just a need to know," she explains. Getting through to her father, who is a very distant, temperamental person, has been difficult, however. And the old fear of rejection surfaced again when she informed him of her plans to go to Korea to search.

"When I told my dad I was going to Korea, I imagined he was going to scream. I didn't know what was going to happen, but I thought he was going to flip out, you know. And to have him flip out and reject me totally was the *scariest* thing!" Although he certainly didn't do that, he wasn't very supportive. His only comment was, "You know how small the chances are of finding anything, don't you?"

A part of the problem was that he just didn't see why finding her birth mother was important. "Sometimes my father doesn't understand why I need to know who she is. So I asked him what it would be like for him not to know who he looked like, or not to know whose traits he had, or not to know where he was born, and to celebrate a birthday that meant nothing to him all his life. And he shut up for a while. Because there's no other way you can explain that your whole life is a mystery," Emily says. "And I have to know from her side, what happened," she adds.

Her mother, on the other hand, felt tremendously threatened. But because Emily had the advantage of being in therapy and in a search group, she knew what to expect and that her mother's reaction was normal.

"Feelings of jealousy, a feeling of anxiety. Like, 'What if she likes this woman more than she likes me? Will she leave me?' It's a fear, and I can understand it."

As an adoptee, Emily relates strongly to the feeling of being abandoned. "Making someone feel abandoned is the *last* thing I want to do, being abandoned myself! I don't want to hurt anybody and put them in the same position I was in.

"I told my mother, 'I love you so much! And the fact that you're helping me shows how much you love me. I'm not going to exchange you for anybody! I just need to know who this woman is.' "

Obviously, an international search such as this poses many more problems than one within the United States. Emily lives in New York, half a world away from Korea. Although records are open in Korea, they aren't necessarily well organized or in good shape. And you need to be able to speak Korean to ask for the information you need.

As a first step, Emily and her mother went to Korea as part of a tour for Koreans who had been adopted by American families. Although everyone on the tour had come to get their personal histories, no one besides Emily was actually trying to locate their family.

Fortunately, because of her mother's job, Emily had access to some very useful contacts. "My mom works at CBS, and a friend of hers called CBS in Korea and asked them to help. They were wonderful! They had someone there to interpret for us.

"We went to the orphanage and they had a picture of me, and they had my name—which is mine, I'm sure. They had my birthday too, but it was clear somebody made this up."

The police station where Emily was abandoned was their next stop. This was possibly the lowest point of her whole time in Korea. Although the police previously had her records, they had discarded them just a few years earlier along with other old papers. "I cried," Emily said, "I cried in front of them! At the orphanage, no, but the police station. I was abandoned at the police station, so that was the last resort. And to find out they had nothing!"

As it turned out, however, it was not their last resort. A contact of her mother's got a small story placed in two Korean newspapers. A TV show saw the article, asked to interview Emily, and did a five-minute piece about her search.

The response was overwhelming—too much for Emily to handle, in fact. Emily's hotel had been listed in the newspapers and the TV show, so that anyone who might have information could contact her. "The phone didn't stop ringing . . . everybody in Seoul called us!" she says. "And they didn't speak English, so it was frustrating. We took down all their numbers, but after a couple of hours, it was so unbearable that we asked the hotel not to let anybody call except for Mr. Han, the guy who was helping us."

The one thing Emily hadn't been prepared for was the flood of Koreans who thought they might be her parents. Meeting some of these people was almost more than she could stand. "It was so scary that I never want to do that again," she says emphatically. " 'Cause I would have believed, *wanted* to believe, anyone. But to be this close, and then not have a birthmark, so I wasn't their daughter, or I wasn't the same age, or they lost a child in the summer, when I was lost in the winter . . . things like that. . . .

"In all my preparation, I didn't think I was going to meet someone who *wasn't* my mother—'either you meet her or you don't,' I thought. So I got there, and I'm meeting these people who were *crying*, and I wanted to be their daughter so bad!"

With each potential reunion, it was the same. "The only way to explain the feeling is that you feel hot and cold at the same time, your stomach is shaking so much that you can't talk without having your voice shake, you feel your heart shaking, almost squeezing. You want to know these people, you want to love them already. It's like you're going to burst, you know.

"And then when you find out it's not them, your whole body just drops," Emily continues. "You feel like you're floating again in space, you're not rooted any-where. It's like being lost again, not having anything concrete. It sounds dramatic, but it's really horrible! After being that close and then not having it again."

Through all of this, Emily's mother was dying inside too. "I know she hurt a lot," Emily says, " 'cause there's no way you can't. I mean, it's overwhelming for her because she has to deal with the fact that this is *real*, it's really happening."

When Emily finally couldn't go on meeting people who might or might not be her birth parents, her mother went instead while Emily stayed in the car. "She must hate me for that," Emily says. "She had to deal with the fact that maybe these were my parents. And that frightened her, I know it frightened her—she told me. We cried a lot on the trip! I cried more than she did, but we both cried."

Right before they were scheduled to leave Korea, Emily and her mother were contacted by a woman who seemed the most likely candidate yet, although they were unable to meet her in person. The woman's daughter has the same name as the one Emily gave the police as a child, and this name is uncommon. Although the woman's daughter would be eight months older than Emily is, there has always been some suspicion that Emily may be older than her records indicated, because her speech was more advanced than that of most children who are the age she was supposed to have been.

The woman was married to a man who was an alcoholic, and he drove her and her three children out of the home. According to the information she supplied, the woman's daughter was left with a neighbor. But because she cried so much, they took her to a police station outside of Seoul. Although it's unclear if this was the same station Emily was left at, it is at least in the same general area. Over time, this daughter was adopted by Americans, as was Emily, another daughter was adopted by a family in Sweden, and the oldest child, a boy, remained in Korea, where he still lives.

The only way to be sure, of course, was to have DNA blood tests done. This was the closest Emily had come to believing that her search might be at an end. For agonizing weeks, Emily awaited the arrival of the woman's blood sample from Korea and then for the test results. Unfortunately, her blood sample didn't match with Emily's. To Emily's great disappointment, the woman was not her mother.

Emily's experience in Korea matured her in many ways, and coming back to her life here, after all she had been through, seemed a little strange. "I'm starting school now, tomorrow—the twelfth grade—and I looked around and I'm like, 'What am I doing with all these kids?' It felt so weird! But I got back into it."

Emily and her mother still have contact with a police officer in Korea who is tracking down the many other leads. But he does this in his spare time, and so far, nothing has materialized.

Has all this pain been for nothing, then? "My therapist asked me, 'If you could go back to Korea and go through everything again, would you?' And I said, 'You bet your life I would!' I feel like I did everything I could have done, everything in my power. And that feels good."

Moreover, she did learn some things about herself—her real name, for example. With her mother's support, she is legally changing her American name to her original Korean name.

While there is still some hope that she will find her birth mother, she realizes this may never happen. But even if she doesn't find her birth mother, in a very real sense she has found her adoptive mother. "The fact that she helped me with this, and that I *know*, I really *know* that she's supporting me in the search, really brought us a lot closer. 'Cause I'm doing this for myself, you know. And to know that she really wants to be a part of this. She wants to be friends with my birth mother. And what more can you ask of your two parents but to be friends. The day we meet her—I mean, can you picture it? It's going to be beautiful!!"

SELENA

Selena was adopted as an infant by a couple who had been advised they would never be able to have children. Although she was told about her adoption when she was very young, this was against her adoptive father's wishes. As Selena recalls, "The adoption agency told my parents that they should tell me I was adopted at the earliest possible age. And my father said, 'No! I don't want her to know. She's my daughter—end of conversation!' " As a result, the agency made her parents sign an agreement stipulating that they would tell her as soon as possible, and they complied.

Initially Selena accepted the idea that, as an adopted child, she was chosen. In fact, she says, "When I was really small, I went around to everyone saying, 'Ha, ha, ha! I'm special, you're not. I'm adopted.' "

But at age five, her life—and her feelings about being adopted—changed abruptly. To her parents' astonishment, her mother became pregnant and the couple had a daughter. Having been told all her life that she would be an only child, Selena now had a younger sister to contend with.

"My sister was born on my mother's birthday, which was a big blow to me," she says. Moreover, Selena's sister looked just like their mother, while Selena's appearance was very different. Selena believes being adopted accentuated the usual problems of an only child adjusting to a new sibling.

"I think being adopted made it more difficult, because my sister is my mother's identical twin. And my mom's mom, my gran. I mean, put the three of them together and they look like triplets. They have dark hair

96

and dark eyes, and here I am with blond hair and green eyes. I definitely stand out in my family."

The worst part, however, was the reaction of some of her father's relatives. "It was like everybody was *so happy*! 'Look! Now we have one of our own!'" Her mother's relatives treat Selena and her sister and brother (who was born later) the same, but the reaction of her father's family is still painful.

Shortly after her sister's birth, Selena's family moved and she entered elementary school. It was around this time that Selena began having problems about being adopted.

"When I was six, I stopped telling people I was adopted. I started feeling like it was a big secret. And then I told someone I trusted, and it was all over the school," she says.

The results were disastrous. As some of the other children told her, "You're not special, you're not chosen. Your mother didn't *want* you."

For the first time Selena realized the implications of being adopted. "To be chosen, somebody had to give you up in the *first* place. I'd never put the two together before," Selena says.

"It was horrible, really horrible," she adds. "And I started having a lot of problems at school. I was always a very hyperactive child, and it just got worse." In an attempt to deal with her difficulties, Selena's parents took her to a doctor who put her on medication. "But within a month, I was like a zombie," she continues.

When that approach proved unsuccessful, Selena was sent to a therapist. But this was doomed from the start. "The person my mother sent me to was the father of one of my classmates. I went to him about three times and never said a word. How could I tell him, 'Hey, your son and all my classmates are giving me problems because I'm adopted, I'm different.' "

As might be expected from her father's initial reaction, adoption was a closed topic in Selena's family. About all her parents would say was that her mother had loved her very much, and that's why she had given her up for adoption. The few details they provided about her were contradictory. "I'd get a lot of mixed-up stories. My father would tell me my mother was an only child, and then my mother would tell me she was from a large family. They couldn't get their stories straight. I think it had a lot to do with how they rationalized it," she said.

With her relatives' elation at having a child "of their own" and her classmates pointing out that she was different, it's no suprise that Selena thought about actively searching for her birth mother at a younger age than most. "From what I remember," she says, "I must have been around eleven, because I was in the sixth grade. I told a couple of my friends that I was adopted and that I wanted to find my birth parents."

Firsthand Experience

While Selena had good relationships with both her parents when she was a child, "When I turned thirteen, I hit the teenage years, and things started to go downhill. I'm not sure how much had to do with the adoption and how much was just your normal teenage rebellion type of thing. I think it was probably half and half," she adds.

"And then, when I was about thirteen, my mother and I got into a fight and I said that I wanted to find my *real* parents." Although she said this in anger, Selena was serious. The problem was, she had no idea how to go about it.

"I'd talk to my friends, and I'd try to think, 'All right, what can I do?' " When she first started discussing it, the laws in her state would have permitted her to get her nonidentifying information at age sixteen. But by the time she reached that age, the law had been changed.

She and her friends tossed around ideas of how she might begin to search, but they didn't get very far. As she recalls, "One of my friends in particular had a computer. And he thought, 'Maybe I can break into the records.' Things like that. And I'm like, 'No, I don't know if I want to go to jail for this yet.' Or I thought, 'Gee, I wonder what kind of research I can do?' But I had no idea how to go about it."

It wasn't until she left home that Selena began her search in earnest. "Finally, I went away to college and that's when I really started trying to figure out what I could do. But even then, I didn't know how to go about getting the nonidentifying information. I didn't know how to do anything." Ironically, there was a search group only a mile and a half from her school, but Selena was unaware of its existence.

A year later, she transferred to a college in a distant state. Strangely, a seemingly casual conversation with her mother at Christmas of that year changed her luck and led to a reunion with her birth mother.

"I had just turned nineteen and I was driving with my mother, and she said something to me like, 'Have you been thinking about searching for your birth mother?' Out of the blue! And I said, 'Yeah, a little.' And that was it.

"Then, about six months later—right before my twentieth birthday—I got a phone call from my mother, telling me about a group in my area that helped adoptees search for their birth parents."

Apparently her mother had been talking to a friend about her own feelings of losing Selena to adulthood. As it happened, he was an adoptive parent, and the conversation turned to the losses involved in adoption. " 'Cause she remembered the fight and maybe a few things that I had said since then," Selena says. "Or the look in my eyes, or just the way I said it—that this is something I wanted to do and I had to do for *me*."

Selena took time off from work and went to the

next meeting of the search group. With their help, she got her nonidentifying information.

Since she lives in a different part of the country than the one in which she grew up, her mother had to do much of the actual searching. The one concrete clue her nonidentifying information provided was the religious affiliation of her birth mother. Since there were only three churches of this denomination in Selena's hometown, she and her mother wrote them asking for information, but they received nothing.

The Social Services Department in her home state has a registry for adoptees that Selena could have joined when she was twenty-one. But through inside contacts, she learned that no one with her mother's matching information was on file.

Up to this point, Selena and her mother had not shared with her father the fact that she was searching because they thought he would be upset. But, as it happened, one of the major TV networks decided to do a program on search groups, and Selena's group was the one they chose to focus on. With the possibility that her father might see the show, Selena realized she had to let him know what she was doing.

"He watched the show," Selena recalls, "and afterwards, he said, 'Two weeks, Selena.' I said, 'What do you mean?' And he said, 'Two weeks. If we had two weeks, I could find her.' "

This from the man who hadn't even wanted her to

be told she was adopted? "I think me being on this TV program and my mother telling him the work that I had been doing showed him how much this really meant to me," she explains. "I think he always knew, but he tried not to show it because he didn't want to lose me," she adds.

The day before her twenty-first birthday, Selena's mother called again. Because they were running out of options, her mother told her that she had put an ad in their hometown paper with Selena's birth date, stating that she was looking for her birth mother to obtain medical information and adding that Selena didn't want to disturb the mother's life. It listed Selena's home phone number and her adoptive mother's number, and mentioned that Selena's adoptive mother was supportive of her search.

Selena and her mother had talked about doing this before, but they were advised by the search group to leave this as a last resort. If she was going to do it, however, they suggested that she pick her birthday or Mother's Day—a time when her birth mother would be thinking of her and might read the personal ads. "But we didn't think it was going to work, to put it very bluntly," Selena says.

"What happened was that one of my birth aunts picked up the paper because she was looking for a baby-sitter for her daughter's kids," Selena recalls. "And she was flipping through the classifieds and she gets to the personals and sees this." Selena's birth mother had stayed with this aunt while she was pregnant, so the aunt knew Selena's birth name and the date and time she was born.

The aunt called Selena's birth mother and asked if this could possibly be the daughter she surrendered. Selena's mother had no doubt that it was.

The following day, on her twenty-first birthday, Selena received a call at nine o'clock in the morning. "And somebody said, 'Can I speak to Selena Wright.' I said 'Speaking.' And she said, 'I'm Betty Hoover and I think I'm your birth mother.'

"Instantly, I was awake!" Selena continues. "I had my nonidentifying information and I said 'Okay, but before we get either one of our hopes up any more, let's go through this.' And everything matched!"

How did she feel? "I was *so incredibly happy!* I mean, I had tears in my eyes—I have tears in my eyes now! It was the best birthday present I could ever have had in my entire life," she says, smiling.

"Then I had to call my parents," she continues. "I called my mom, and my mom's at work and starts to cry. And she said, 'You've got to call your daddy.' So I called my father and said, 'Dad, guess what? I found my birth mother.' It was the first time in my entire life I ever heard my father speechless. He didn't say anything for about a minute. And I said, 'Dad! Dad! Are you okay?' And he answered, 'I'm sitting here crying.' "

Selena and her birth mother, Betty, then made plans to get together in person. Shortly after Selena's birth, Betty met her future husband, to whom she is still married. From the very beginning, Betty told him about Selena. Since they married only six months after Selena's birth, they had considered trying to get her back. But they didn't have the money for a lawyer and were afraid of what could happen to them legally if they tried to find her. Also they were reluctant to upset Selena's life with her new family, so they abandoned the idea. The fact that Betty's husband had known about Selena's existence from the beginning, however, meant fewer complications for the reunion.

As an outgrowth of the television program on her search group, another program wished to tape Selena's reunion with Betty. Because of the number of family members—hers and Betty's—and the TV crew, they decided to meet at Selena's parents' house, which was larger. Also, as Selena puts it, "I wanted to be on my turf."

The reunion was a very positive experience for Selena, although as might be expected, it was a little awkward initially. "I think it was [because it was] the first meeting—like a date. Whether you like the person or not, you're very uncomfortable for the first few minutes," Selena says.

It was also strange to see her face reflected in someone else's. "What was difficult was looking into her

Firsthand Experience

face and seeing me, because we look a lot alike. And for someone who's never had anyone she looked like, it was very bizarre—very, very strange."

Selena's parents and Betty liked each other, which also made things go much smoother. And Selena had a chance to learn why her mother surrendered her for adoption. "She and my birth father had parted way before she even knew she was pregnant. When she called and told him, he said, 'I don't believe you and even if you are, it's not mine.' " Without the resources to support a baby, Selena's mother relinquished her for adoption.

Selena would like to find her birth father as well. But, unfortunately, her mother was so traumatized by his rejection that she completely blocked out his last name. This means that Selena will have to start all over to search for him.

The only difficulty Selena has encountered in her reunion with her birth mother has been with Betty's oldest daughter, Tamara. Although both Tamara and her younger sister, Judy, have always known about Selena, her actual appearance in their lives was a shock. "The older one, Tamara, she and I don't get along so well," Selena says. "I've met her once and a couple of times I've talked to her on the phone, and she just hands the phone to Betty. I think she feels I'm usurping, taking her place. It's that she feels like number one, and I'm taking her place as the oldest." But according to Betty, Tamara also believes that Selena doesn't like her, "So I think it's also some lack of communication on both parts," Selena admits.

Selena and Betty's relationship is still evolving. "We're really good friends," she says. "I mean, I can't really have another mother. It's tough though. We have our moments when we go through a mother-daughter thing, but I'm almost twenty-two years old, and I really don't even have a mothering relationship with my adoptive mother anymore—it's more friends. And that's what you end up with if you're an adult.

"It's a growing process, and we're still getting to know each other. We've got twenty-one years to make up—though they're never going to be made up, unfortunately, because of everything."

Like Chloe, Emily, and most adoptees who have had their parents' support in searching, Selena has grown much closer to her adoptive mother. "Yeah, to me, it's very bizarre," she says. "Because here's this lady I didn't get along with, I *really* didn't get along with *a lot* during high school. We were constantly at each other's throats. But since I started searching, my mother and I have grown really close. Like I can talk to her about almost anything, and I used to [not be able to]. I just couldn't. And now she is just like one of my best friends. I love it!" she adds with a smile.

Chloe, Emily, Selena, and the others whose experiences have been presented here decided that it was important for them to search. Like them, you may want to find your birth parents as well. On the other hand, you may not wish to search or are unsure as to how you feel about this issue right now. Regardless of what you decide to do, however, it is your *right* to know the details of your own history and to connect to your biological and cultural roots, if you want to. Fortunately, adoptees, birth parents, adoptive parents, and the general public are becoming increasingly aware that— whatever your decision—the choice should be yours.

In Search Of

ONE of the first things adoptees and birth parents who are searching learn is that it's important to take advantage of any and every opportunity that presents itself. Thus, some of the adoptees and birth parents to whom we spoke while writing this book have asked that their identifying information or the information on those for whom they are looking be listed here. They know the odds are small that the right person may see this notice and contact them. But, as Selena's experience illustrates, even a long shot works out once in a while.

If you are one of the individuals listed on the following two pages, are looking for one of these people, or have any information that may be helpful in locating any of them, please contact Adoption Crossroads, New York City, (212) 988-0110.

In Search Of

Adoptee Date of Birth	Adoptee City of Birth	Name
11/03/39 (?)	New York, N.Y. (?)	Birth Name: Robert Wilson Birth Mother: Ruth Haverman or Ruth Habersack Adopted Name: Joe Soll
1/27/67	Toronto, Canada	Birth Name: (Baby Girl) Jones
1/29/70	New York, N.Y.	Birth Name: (Baby Boy) Eaton
1972, 1973, or 1974	Seoul, Korea	Birth Name: Eun Joo Kim (Female)
12/11/62	Miami, Fla.	Adopted Name: Leah Rollhaus
4/05/57	Bayonne, N.J.	Adopted Name: Jane Simoni
6/28/68	New York, N.Y.	Adopted Name: Berrie Hodge Birth Mother: May Phillips
2/27/66	New York, N.Y.	Birth Name: Mary McNamara

In Search Of

3/06/77	New York, N.Y.	Birth Name: John David Kleinholz
		Adopted Name: John Volk Blum
3/31/53	Van Nuys, Calif.	Birth Name: (Female) Chamousis
		Adopted Name: Katina Demetra
12/13/48	Brooklyn, N.Y.	Birth Name: David (?) Wolf
		Adopted Name: Philip Millstein
12/31/65	Brooklyn, N.Y.	Birth Name: (Female) Hall
		Adopted Name: Geralynn F. Gatto
11/13/44	New York, N.Y. Misericordia Hospital	Birth Name: Martha Patricia Rafinski
		Adopted Name: Caroline Marie Tryskuc
(Date of Abandonment) 10/02/63	(Place of Abandonment) Bond Hotel Chambers Street New York, N.Y.	Adopted Name: Richard Stark Birth Mother: Dorothy Peterson (Philadelphia)

For More Information

SEARCH AND SUPPORT GROUPS
NATIONAL ORGANIZATIONS

Search and support groups exist throughout the country. Because local meeting places change frequently, the best way to find a group is through the national organizations listed below. They will be happy to refer you to a group in your area.

Council for Equal Rights in Adoption
401 East 74th Street
New York, NY 10021-3919
212-988-0110
(Over 320 locations in 8 countries)

For More Information

Concerned United Birthparents
2000 Walker Street
Des Moines, IA 50317
800-822-2777
(30 locations in 2 countries)

Orphan Voyage
2141 Road 2300
Cedaredge, CO 81413
303-856-3937
(The oldest organization. Has 6 locations)

REGISTRY

Birthparents, adoptees, and adoptive parents acting in behalf of their adopted children may register with:

International Soundex Reunion Registry
P.O. Box 2312
Carson City, NV 89702-2313
702-882-7755

For Further Reading

Jeanne DuPrau. *The Facts, Feelings, and Issues of a Double Heritage: Adoption.* New York: Julian Messner, 1990.

Jill Krementz. *How It Feels to Be Adopted.* New York: Alfred A. Knopf, 1982.

Betty Jean Lifton. *Lost and Found: The Adoption Experience.* New York: Harper and Row, 1988.

Steven Nickman. *The Adoption Experience.* New York: Julian Messner, 1985.

Paul Sachdev. *Unlocking the Adoption Files.* Toronto: Lexington Books, 1989.

Arthur Sorosky, Annette Baran, and Reuben Pannor. *The Adoption Triangle.* New York: Anchor Press/Doubleday, 1987.

John Triseliotis. *In Search of Origins: The Experiences of Adopted People.* New York: Routledge and Kegan Paul, 1973.

SEARCH BOOKS

There are several books on the market that deal at length with specific search techniques and procedures.

Although they offer an enormous amount of information, these books have limited usefulness, in part because most people are overwhelmed and confused by this much detail. Even more important, these books rarely enable you to uncover a critical missing piece in your search—your birth name.

While it is highly unlikely that you can successfully search using just these books, they can provide you with helpful ideas and resources for tracking down a birth parent once you have your birth name. Even so, you will probably need guidance to use these suggestions effectively.

Four of these books are listed here. Publishing company addresses are provided for books that may be difficult to find in a bookstore so that you can order them directly.

Jane Askin. *Search: A Handbook for Adoptees and Birthparents*, second edition. Phoenix: Oryx Press, 1992. (Oryx Press, 4041 North Central and Indian School Road, Phoenix, Arizona 85012)

Ted Gunderson. *How to Locate Anyone Anywhere Without Leaving Home*. New York: E. P. Dutton, 1989.

Mary Jo Rillera. *The Adoption Searchbook: Techniques for Tracing People*. Westminster, California: Triadoption Publications, 1991. (Triadoption Publications, P.O. Box 638, Westminster, California 32684)

Joan A. S. Strauss. *The Great American Search Book*. Worcester, Massachusetts: Castle Rock Publishing Company, 1990. (Castle Rock Publishing Company, P.O. Box 161, Worcester, Massachusetts 01602)

Index

117

Index

Index

Groundedness, sense of, 18

Identifying information, 84, 109
Identity
  establishing, 20
  sense of, 12
Illegitimacy, 9
Infertility, 19
Information
  see Identifying information;
    Nonidentifying information
International adoptions, 42–43,
  85–95

Korea, 42, 85–95

Loss
  in adoption, 10
  sense of, 16
Love, 6, 27
  for/of birth mother, 71–72
  in birth mother, 65, 66

Medical history, 7, 43

Nonidentifying information, 37–
  38, 39, 40, 84, 99, 100, 101,
  103
Nurturing, 66–67

Parental permission, need for, 38
Personal ads, 102–3
Physical resemblance
  to birth mother, 104–5
  lack of, 65, 77–78, 86, 97
Postreunion, 64–75
Problems in living, 13
Psychotherapy, 31, 36, 87, 88, 89,
  98

Race, 3
Rage, 67–68
  see also Anger
Rebelliousness, 9
Registry(ies), 21, 38–39, 45, 58,
  101, 125
Regression, 66–67
Rejection, 2, 35, 63, 82, 84
  by birth mother, 47–49
  of birth mother, 54–56
  fear of, 20–21, 22, 33, 49, 50,
    63, 88, 89
  feelings of, in adoptive parents,
    17
Relationship(s)
  with adoptive parents, 16–17,
    23, 24–26, 83, 87, 88, 89, 99
  with birth mother, 60–61, 62,
    64, 66, 71–75, 85, 106
  with family, 35
  problems with, 8–9
Reunion(s), ix, 30, 56, 63, 64–75,
  84, 104–6
  with birth mothers, 54–63
  potential, 92–94
Right to know, 107

Search/support groups, 21, 23,
  30–36, 45, 62–63, 66, 79–81,
  83, 89, 100, 101, 102, 104
  birth mothers in, 33–35, 66, 80–
    81
  foreign, 126
  locating, 36
  national organizations, 116–17
  by state, 118–26
Search techniques/strategies, 31,
  35, 43
Search(ing)
  for birth fathers, 61–62

119

Index